Formation for Transformation

Formation for Transformation

Ecumenical Reception through Ecumenical Formation

Bruce Myers

Foreword by Linda Nicholls

WIPF & STOCK · Eugene, Oregon

FORMATION FOR TRANSFORMATION
Ecumenical Reception through Ecumenical Formation

Copyright © 2022 Bruce Myers. All rights reserved. Except for brief quotations in critical publications or reviews, no part of this book may be reproduced in any manner without prior written permission from the publisher. Write: Permissions, Wipf and Stock Publishers, 199 W. 8th Ave., Suite 3, Eugene, OR 97401.

Wipf & Stock
An Imprint of Wipf and Stock Publishers
199 W. 8th Ave., Suite 3
Eugene, OR 97401

www.wipfandstock.com

PAPERBACK ISBN: 978-1-6667-2908-5
HARDCOVER ISBN: 978-1-6667-2091-4
EBOOK ISBN: 978-1-6667-2092-1

01/10/22

To all of my ecumenical friends

[E]cumenism, the movement promoting Christian unity, is not just some sort of "appendix" which is added to the church's traditional activity. Rather, ecumenism is an organic part of her life and work, and consequently must pervade all that she is and does; it must be like the fruit borne by a healthy and flourishing tree which grows to its full stature.
—POPE JOHN PAUL II

Ecumenism is not an extra that one can fit in because it's an interesting occupation. It is the oxygen of mission and evangelism.
—ARCHBISHOP OF CANTERBURY JUSTIN WELBY

Contents

List of Tables | ix
Foreword by Linda Nicholls | xi
Acknowledgements | xiii
Abbreviations | xv

Introduction | 1
1 Reception | 13
2 Ecumenical Theological Education | 32
3 Transformative Learning | 70
4 Surveying Canadian Anglican Ecumenical Formation | 89
5 A Proposed Revised Practice | 126

Conclusion | 158

Bibliography | 167
Index | 177

List of Tables

1. Comparison of suggestions for practical ecumenical engagement included in *Growing Together in Unity and Mission*, *A Handbook of Spiritual Ecumenism*, and *Christian Unity: How You Can Make a Difference* | 60–7
2. Percentage of TST basic degree students staying in home college | 106

Foreword

ALTHOUGH I AM A cradle Anglican, early experiences of interdenominational formation deeply shaped the understanding of my faith. Whether through experiences as a young musician serving a Presbyterian church; as a theological student sharing in a multi-denominational theological federation; or as a young priest invited to join the Anglican-Roman Catholic Dialogue in Canada, I discovered the gifts and grace present in traditions other than my own. Even as I knew we all shared a core common Christian identity and commitment I came to appreciate the particular gifts of different theological perspectives, denominational structure, and emphases in worship and appreciated my own tradition in new ways. Later experiences in ordained ministry of ecumenical sharing in worship, refugee sponsorship, shared ministries, international ecumenical dialogue, and full communion partnership enriched my understanding of my own tradition, its strengths and weaknesses, and shaped my vision for the one, holy, catholic church. They also taught me the ground rules for listening deeply to the other, to explore and understand differences and heal inappropriate stereotypes, while building bridges in community. Looking back, I cannot imagine what my ministry would have looked like without the gift of ecumenical experiences and formation.

Bishop Bruce Myers recognizes the importance of this kind of ecumenical formation in the life of the church, not as an academic exercise of interest, but as critical area of preparation for ministry that is needed, often neglected or often only honored in the breach. It is formation that happens informally through contact, relationships, shared ministry, and shared worship in addition to the formal opportunities of intentional reflection, learning and dialogue. It is rooted in experiences of transformational learning like those that formed my own ministry.

Bishop Myers explores the roots of ecumenical commitments at the judicatory level of churches, where theological agreements have been discerned, and then examines how this has, or has not, reached into the church—especially into the lives of those who give leadership as clergy and in the lived practice of the church.

He takes an honest look at the current state of theological education in Canada to assess its capacity for ecumenical formation, finding that though it is valued it is difficult to deliver in a fulsome way. To truly be transformative in one's own life and ministry it must move from intellectual assent to doctrinal propositions to lived experience that engages the whole person; from the agreed statements of an ecumenical commission to local churches engaged in mission together. It must be embedded in the intentions of every aspect of formation for ministry, academic, practical and pastoral.

As a judicatory leader seeing the challenges of both institutional decline and post-pandemic issues, the urgency of being familiar with our ecumenical partners in mission and ministry, and knowledge of agreed statements and ecclesial understandings, will be heightened. The silos of denominational life that thrived during Christendom have crumbled, particularly in more rural and isolated parts of Canada. When asked about sharing worship and ministry with an ecumenical partner many declining congregations shy away as the needed ecumenical formation that could see the other as a partner rather than a competitor has not yet happened. The saddest moments of episcopal ministry are to watch a congregation choose to die rather than engage creatively with an ecumenical partner. It is essential that the clergy leadership be formed and ready to consider such shifts and to guide congregations in ecumenical sharing that witnesses holistically to our life in Christ first and our denominational label secondarily.

It is my hope that theological colleges, diocesan discernment and formation committees, post-ordination training programs, and lay education will all pay attention to this call for renewed commitment to ecumenical formation as essential to the health of the church, the one, holy, catholic and apostolic church gathered in the name of the Trinity for worship and service.

The Most Rev. Linda Nicholls
Primate, Anglican Church of Canada
July 7, 2021

Acknowledgements

I OWE DEBTS OF gratitude to the many individuals and organizations that helped make the completion of this research project not only possible, but also thoroughly enjoyable—both in its initial form as a doctor of ministry dissertation at Saint Paul University in Ottawa, and subsequently as the volume you are now reading.

Several supportive colleagues helped create the time and space necessary for me to conduct this work. At the General Synod of the Anglican Church of Canada these included Eileen Scully, Michael Thompson, and Fred Hiltz. In the Anglican Diocese of Quebec, I am especially grateful to Edward Simonton and Marie-Sol Gaudreau.

Mitzi Budde provided me with what turned out to be pivotal access to her own doctor of ministry dissertation, and also served as a highly engaged external examiner. Linda Nicholls, who offers the foreword to this book, served as my "on-site mentor" as a part of the doctor of ministry program.

Kevin Flynn and the Anglican community at Saint Paul University welcomed me into their worship and fellowship while I sojourned on campus, and Tyler Burke generously shared his home and table with me during my study visits to Ottawa. My mother, Marion Myers, also always had a meal and bed at the ready for when I'd be passing through Glengarry County, Ontario, on my way to or from time at Saint Paul. Neil Alexander and the School of Theology at the University of the South in Sewanee, Tennessee, also generously extended their hospitality to me as a bishop-in-residence, during which time I was able to engage in some intensive research and writing.

I'm also grateful to the dozens of fellow clergy from across the Anglican Church of Canada—especially the heads of our church's centers of theological formation—who took the time and effort to so fulsomely complete the surveys that provide the raw data for this research. Holly Ratcliffe helped me respect the demands of the university's Research Ethics Board by collating surveys submitted by clergy under my direct oversight.

The team at Wipf and Stock made my first dive into the world of book publishing a delight. I'm especially grateful to Matthew Wimer for his patient guidance throughout the process.

Generous financial support for this research and its subsequent publication has been received with gratitude from the Anglican Foundation of Canada, the Continuing Education Plan of the Anglican Church of Canada, Saint Paul University, the Anglican Diocese of Quebec, the Oratory of the Good Shepherd, the Toronto Commandery of the Order of Saint Lazarus, and the Primate of the Anglican Church of Canada.

Jeffrey Metcalfe and John Gibaut were each in their own way influential and encouraging in my decision to engage in this research in the first place, to pursuit it through the doctor of ministry program at Saint Paul University, and to stick with it after I was called to a new and demanding ministry in midstream.

I also extend my thanks to the members of my thesis committee, Miriam Martin, Yvan Mathieu, and especially my thesis director, Catherine Clifford, for their interest, engagement, availability, and support throughout this longer-than-expected endeavor.

Abbreviations

ARCIC	Anglican-Roman Catholic International Commission
AST	Atlantic School of Theology
ATS	Association of Theological Schools in the United States and Canada
CCC	Canadian Council of Churches
CTS	Conference of Theological Seminaries
ELCA	Evangelical Lutheran Church in America
ELCIC	Evangelical Lutheran Church in Canada
ESM	Ecumenical shared ministry
GTUM	*Growing Together in Unity and Mission*
IARCCUM	International Anglican-Roman Catholic Commission on Unity and Mission
IASCER	Inter-Anglican Standing Commission on Ecumenical Relations
JDDJ	Joint Declaration on the Doctrine of Justification
JWG	Joint Working Group between the Roman Catholic Church and the World Council of Churches
LWF	Lutheran World Federation
MDiv	Master of Divinity
PCPCU	Pontifical Council for Promoting Christian Unity
TEAC	Theological Education in the Anglican Communion
TST	Toronto School of Theology
VST	Vancouver School of Theology
WCC	World Council of Churches

Introduction

SINCE THE EARLY TWENTIETH century many historic mainline churches, such as the Anglican Church of Canada to which I belong, have been engaged in formal theological conversations with other churches. These conversations can be said to have as their goal "a restoration of complete communion of faith and sacramental life" of the participating churches so that they might "strive in common to find solutions for all the great problems that face those who believe in Christ in the world of today."[1] Put another way, for those churches that articulate it as a priority, participation in the ecumenical movement is necessary because Christian division compromises the credibility of the church's witness and renders less effective the church's reconciling mission in and for the world.

In the contemporary Canadian context, the need for a more visible and tangible unity among the churches is still more acute. The secular age which the churches in Canada (and elsewhere) inhabit has generally resulted in consistently declining membership and diminishing financial resources. From a practical standpoint, a failure by churches to engage ecumenically results in an inefficient division and duplication of resources. From a public witness standpoint, divided churches failing to be in dialogue and common mission with each other compromise their credibility. From a pluralistic standpoint, fruitful and peaceful dialogue with the increasing number of adherents of other religions present in Canada is complicated by the Christian churches's incapacity to speak with one voice. From a theological standpoint, ecumenism is nothing less than a gospel imperative, Jesus Christ himself having exhorted his followers to eschew their divisions for the sake of his reconciling mission, "that they may all be one" (John 17:21).

1. Pope Paul VI and Archbishop Michael Ramsay, "Common Declaration."

Formation for Transformation

Notwithstanding the impressive level of formal theological agreement achieved in the past several decades, the degree to which that agreement has been accepted and integrated into the lives of the churches involved (or, to use a technical term, the degree to which that agreement has been *received* by the churches) has been called into doubt.[2] A whole area of scholarship has emerged to address this question of ecumenical reception: "the need for translation of theological agreements into practical actions in the churches."[3] There is a consensus within this scholarly community that in general this task of translation largely remains to be done, though models to promote ecumenical reception are emerging. However, the basis for this consensus seems largely anecdotal or assumed, and little exists in the way of statistical or qualitative evidence.

In the several decades that the Anglican Church of Canada has been engaged in formal ecumenical conversations, there has been no systematic analysis or review of the degree to which the local expressions of the church (i.e. congregations and the clergy who serve them) are aware of and have received the fruits of these church-to-church dialogues. This denomination has officially and repeatedly identified ecumenical engagement as one of its priorities, but has never clearly assessed the ways in which this priority has (or has not) been respected. Therefore, this study is primarily aimed at assisting the Anglican Church of Canada in determining the extent to which it is (or is not) actually giving tangible expression to those engagements with other churches, especially locally, and in determining whether a revision of its practice in this respect is necessary. At a very basic level, this research will help determine whether the denomination's actions match its stated intentions and attempt to determine why. The critical reflection on the church's practice which is at the heart of this research makes it particularly well suited for the methods of practical theology.

The reception of any teaching, policy, or initiative within the Anglican Church of Canada (and many other Christian denominations) depends in large part on the receptiveness of its ordained leadership. For Anglicans, the orders of priests and bishops have particular responsibility for the pastoral, educational, and administrative leadership of the local churches.

---

2. For example, Colin Buchanan has argued that the vaunted agreement on the understanding of the Eucharist achieved by the Anglican-Roman Catholic International Commission in 1971 has never been received by either communion, in either the juridical or spiritual sense. These distinctions will be discussed in chapter 1. See Buchanan, *Did the Anglicans and Roman Catholics Agree*.

3. Rusch, *Ecumenical Reception*, 54.

Introduction

Therefore, any study of the degree to which ecumenical agreements in the Anglican Church of Canada have been received will need to pay particular attention to this group. The bishops are especially important in this respect since they ultimately determine who will serve as priests in their respective jurisdictions, and sometimes also direct the choice of institution at which prospective priests will train. The bishops are also normally instrumental in establishing the orientations and priorities that priests under their oversight will follow while serving the local churches.

My governing claim therefore is that there exists a relationship between the manner and content of the formation of the clergy of the Anglican Church of Canada and their subsequent knowledge of and commitment to ecumenism. Those who, for example, studied as seminarians with students and instructors of other Christian traditions will as priests or bishops be more naturally inclined to work collaboratively with individuals and groups from other churches, and promote ecumenical engagement in their parishes, dioceses, and in the life of the church in general.

After demonstrating this claim, the practical theological method demands a further step in the hermeneutical process: the proposing of a suggested revised practice emerging from the results of the research. I will therefore also explore the methods and curricula of the institutions at which most Canadian Anglican clergy study, to see if their context and content adequately reflect the ecumenical expectations of the church they are being prepared to serve.

I seek to offer a twofold contribution by way of this research: (1) to the field of ecumenical studies I hope to provide a unique, detailed, and credible evaluation of one church's challenges *vis-à-vis* ecumenical reception, particularly as it pertains to the question of the ecumenical formation of clergy; and (2) to the Anglican Church of Canada I hope to offer concrete strategies and tangible tools to assist it in living into its own stated commitment "to encourage and equip all in the church to walk the way of ecumenism, so that all will come to know the hope for the restoration of the full visible unity of Christ's church."[4]

Context

When I began this research as a doctor of ministry candidate, I was serving as the Anglican Church of Canada's lead national staff person for

---

4. General Synod, "Towards a Renewed Ecumenical Strategy."

ecumenical relations. In that role I was daily confronted with the challenges of ecumenical reception, and perhaps more than any other person in our denomination became acutely aware of the gap that exists between our church's official commitment to ecumenical engagement and the lived-out reality, especially locally. Although I only served in that role for a few years, it was enough time to appreciate the limited extent to which the fruits of many of our church's various ecumenical dialogues—which have often offered practical, concrete suggestions on how divided Christians can live and work in a more visible kind of unity—have been received at the congregational or diocesan level. Awareness of our ecumenical agreements and their implications, even among theologically educated clergy, seemed minimal. I detected a pressing need to foster a higher awareness and better integration into our church's life of existing ecumenical agreements, perhaps even before attempting to negotiate new interchurch accords.

An analogy from my native Ottawa Valley's rich history in the lumber trade may help illustrate the situation. Rather than add more timbers to an existing logjam of ecumenical agreed statements, there is a growing recognition that ecumenists in the current context need to be less like lumberjacks (those who toil in forests downing trees) than log drivers (those who nimbly guide the logs downriver), equipped with the skills to help dislodge extant agreed statements and nimbly navigate them through sometimes choppy waters so they can be received and processed by the churches, and become an integral part of their lives and structures. The finest cut of timber is only of so much use if it is stuck in a bottleneck upriver from the sawmill.

What the analogy attempts to point to is the issue of reception. Whether freshly cut pine timber or a carefully crafted agreed statement on ecclesiology, to be effective the good in question needs to come into the possession of its intended recipient in such a way that it is translated into something tangible—a supporting beam or a mutual recognition of ministry, for example. Increasingly my research and firsthand experience as an ecumenical officer led me to conclude that a significant part of this ecumenical logjam is situated in the seminaries and theological colleges where a large proportion of our church's priests are formed. I therefore came to understand a significant part of my role within the Anglican Church of Canada to be that of an agent of ecumenical reception—an ecumenical log driver, if you will.

Such a role was perhaps obvious during my time as the Anglican Church of Canada's ecumenical officer. However, when after a few years

Introduction

I was called to serve as a bishop, this particular vocation to unity simply took on a different form. A bishop is a "focus and agent of unity," both within their own particular church and the wider *ecclesia*.[5] At my episcopal ordination, among the solemn promises I made was to "promote peace and reconciliation in the church" and to "strive for the visible unity of Christ's church." Therefore, even though I changed orders, locations, and ministries midway through this research project, my vocation to unity remained unchanged, and the ends of this study were at least as germane as before.

State of the Question

The issue at the heart of this research is a perceived—but until now uncorroborated by research—disconnect between the Anglican Church of Canada's stated commitment to ecumenical engagement and the denomination's actual lived experience in this respect, especially in the regional (i.e., diocesan) and local (i.e., congregational) expressions of the church.

The denomination's national expressions have long held up interchurch collaboration as an ideal, at least twice officially committing the Anglican Church of Canada to the ecumenical movement's prime directive, the Lund Principle, which exhorts churches to "act together in all matters except those in which deep differences of conviction compel them to act separately."[6] The General Synod, the Anglican Church of Canada's highest governing body, reaffirmed its commitment to ecumenical engagement through its adoption in 2004 of a little-known declaration called "Towards a Renewed Ecumenical Strategy." Among other things it states that Canadian Anglicans believe they are called "to encourage and equip all in the church to walk the way of ecumenism, so that all will come to know the hope for the restoration of the full visible unity of Christ's church."[7] Still more importantly, the 2010 General Synod stated that to "be leaders in . . . ecumenical actions" was to be one of the denomination's seven top priorities in the decade to follow.

One way this commitment has been expressed is through formal church-to-church dialogues. The Anglican Church of Canada is currently engaged in such official conversations with the Roman Catholic Church, the United Church of Canada, Mennonite Church Canada, and the Moravian

---

5. Avis, *Becoming a Bishop*, 95.
6. West, "Lund Principle," 714–15.
7. General Synod, "Towards a Renewed Ecumenical Strategy."

Church. Years of similar talks with the Evangelical Lutheran Church in Canada (and its antecedents) resulted in the establishment of a relationship of full communion between the two churches in 2001.[8]

However, for all the official ecumenical affirmations made by the national level of the Anglican Church of Canada—separately or as a result of agreements with other denominations with which we are in dialogue—they are only effective if they are received by and lived into by the more local expressions of the church. It more often seems as if at the local level, many Anglican churches live out the Lund Principle in reverse: acting separately in all matters except those in which they are compelled to work together.

Transcending the national-local divide has been a challenge for the General Synod since its earliest days, not least of all because the most frequent and important expression of the Anglican Church of Canada that most of its members will encounter is their local congregation (even if Anglican ecclesiology would identify the diocese, gathered around its bishop, as the primary expression of the church). This is why the theological question at the heart of this research is one of reception, and this will be explored in some depth in the first chapter.

Despite the development of an ever-growing corpus of agreed statements, joint declarations, and commitments to work collaboratively, even ecumenically inclined churches continue to work in relative isolation from one another. While scholars stop short of declaring an outright failure of ecumenical reception, "it is widely recognized that, on most fronts, the aspiration for programmed structural unity in the short-medium term is simply unrealistic,"[9] and that formal ecumenical agreed statements find relatively little purchase in the pastoral practice and lives of local congregations.

What appears to be largely absent from the literature in this area is any attempt to measure this apparent lack of ecumenical reception in any quantifiable way. Most of the literature speaks in general and lamenting ways about how the past generation's aspirations for ecumenical progress have failed to be met. Few concrete or measurable examples are offered, however. What evidence there is appears largely to be anecdotal: for example, the very general observation that in Canada, "Locally, churches could do a lot more together."[10] Such assertions are very likely true, but little in the way of evidence has been collected and analyzed to test their veracity.

8. General Synod, "Bilateral dialogues."
9. Murray, "Receptive Ecumenism and Catholic Learning," 9.
10. Hodgson, "Ecumenical Education," 23.

Introduction

One notable exception is research conducted by a Nigerian Roman Catholic priest and graduate student, who attempted to measure "ecumenical consciousness" among pastoral workers in a particular region of his church. Engaging both quantitative and qualitative research methods, using surveys and interviews, he was able to measure the degree of awareness, acceptance, and implementation of Catholic ecumenical principles among local church workers, concluding, among other things, that "more work is needed in the province to awaken the consciousness of Christian unity in the spirit of *aggiornamento* of Vatican II."[11] He then proceeded to propose strategies proper to his context to address this measurable lack of ecumenical consciousness among church workers, some of which involve proposals for a more robust ecumenical pastoral and theological formation. Closer to home, an attempt was made in 1998 "to examine the state of ecumenical education in terms of Canada in terms of how ecumenism is being 'taught' in theological faculties and institutes around the country."[12] Though many of its findings are revealing and to some extent germane to this research, the survey's scope was broader than that which I intend, the response rate was relatively low, and the results are decades old.

Nevertheless, both of these other pieces of research point to what many have identified as one of the essential elements in the promotion of ecumenical reception: ecumenical formation. The need to inculcate individuals and communities with an ecumenical consciousness is crucial if the revealing of the visible unity of the one church is to remain a priority of the divided churches. In an essay entitled "What Will It Take to Revitalize the Ecumenical Movement?" the noted American ecumenist Michael Kinnamon counted ecumenical formation as a priority: "[I]f the [ecumenical] movement is to have a future, then a new generation of leaders must be grasped by this idea of the church as a sign of wholeness and reconciliation."[13]

This instillation of an ecumenical spirit needs to occur among the whole people of God, laity and clergy. However, because of their particular vocation as teachers and leaders in the church, it is especially crucial that ecumenical formation be a priority in the training of bishops and priests. The Joint Working Group between the Roman Catholic Church and the World Council of Churches has over the years been particularly insistent on this point, calling on the churches to ensure their seminaries teach both

---

11. Anokwulu, *Ecumenical Imperative*, 103.
12. Dowd, "Ecumenical Education in Canada," 25.
13. Kinnamon, *Can a Renewal Movement Be Renewed*, 155.

a specific course on ecumenism and also demonstrate the ecumenical dimension in every other discipline of theology: "Both are part of ecumenical formation, so that ecumenism is not seen as an isolated specialty, but exists as a living component in all theological discourse. Ecumenical formation must be an essential element for candidates for ordained ministry."[14] That the Joint Working Group and the World Council of Churches have each continually drawn attention to the crucial nature of ecumenical formation to ecumenical reception since at least the 1980s suggests there remains work to be done.

While there exists a growing corpus of literature on the question of ecumenical reception, and on the related matter of ecumenical formation, nothing resembling a study or measure of ecumenical consciousness has ever been conducted among Canadian Anglicans, let alone clergy. This research provides for the first time some quantifiable evidence for a lack of reception of ecumenical agreements and initiatives among the ordained leadership of the Anglican Church of Canada, and the particular role played in this respect by the denomination's various training schemes for clergy. The resulting data allows an analysis of the causes of this lack of ecumenical awareness and engagement, and creates the prospect of proposing revised practices to remedy this deficiency.

Methodology

More details with respect to the content and conduct of this research's data collection methods are provided in chapter 4, but a brief outline is provided here. A mixture of quantitative and qualitative research methods was employed through the use of an online survey instrument that permitted both closed and open-ended questions. Two sets of surveys were conducted to test the hypothesis's claim that there exists a link between the context and content of a cleric's theological and pastoral formation and his or her subsequent ecumenical engagement or consciousness.

Two populations of individuals were solicited to participate voluntarily in this study. One group consisted of deacons, priests, and bishops of the Anglican Church of Canada. The other consisted of the principals (or other designated representatives) of theological colleges, seminaries, or other training schemes through which most Anglican clergy in Canada receive their primary theological and pastoral formation for ordination. Excluded

14. Joint Working Group, *Reception*, 61.

Introduction

from consideration were the heads of theological colleges or seminaries outside of Canada. Candidates for ordination in the Anglican Church of Canada occasionally train in such institutions, but their numbers are negligible and would take the study beyond a chiefly Canadian scope.

The clergy survey solicited information concerning their ecumenical interest and engagement before, during, and following their formal seminary training. A significant portion of the survey was dedicated to seeking information about the context and content of their theological and pastoral training, and to their current ecumenical engagement and that of the jurisdictions they oversee.

The survey for the theological college or seminary heads asked them to provide information about, for example, the context of the institution they serve (e.g., does it have any affiliation with schools of other denominations?), teaching methods, field education programs, non-Anglican representation on the faculty, the specific content of the institution's curriculum for those preparing for ordination, the nature of the school's liturgical life and extracurricular fellowship—all with the intention of establishing to what extent each institution's life can be said to have an ecumenical orientation.

The main analytical task concerning the data collected through the surveys was to determine whether they point to a positive relationship between the context and content of a cleric's theological and pastoral formation and their later ecumenical engagement. This might be demonstrated, for example, by a priest who is actively engaged ecumenically in his or her work and who attended a seminary that is part of an ecumenical consortium, who studied, worshiped, and socialized regularly with students of other ecclesial traditions, and who was exposed in his or her seminary's curriculum to theologians and traditions of other churches.

Practical Theology and the Hermeneutical 'Spiral'

The way of proceeding outlined above seeks to follow the fourfold hermeneutical "spiral" that has become a standard methodology of practical theological inquiry. As a discipline of theology that interprets the church's practices, practical theology interprets not simply for the sake of analysis, but so that the church's practices in relation to the world might be adapted or changed—in the light of this interpretation and analysis—so as to allow the church "to participate faithfully in God's mission."[15] As a result, the aim

15. Swinton and Mowat, *Practical Theology*, 27.

of practical theology is "not simply to understand the world but also to change it."[16] In this respect, practical theology's approach lends itself well to the goals of this research project.

The method's four movements have been articulated in slightly different ways by various practical theologians, but this proposal employs the terms and definitions established by Richard Osmer: the *descriptive-empirical task*, the *interpretive task*, the *normative task*, and the *pragmatic task*.[17] Explicitly recasting this particular research project along those lines might therefore resemble the following:

1. *Descriptive-empirical:* Establishing the context of this research and collecting data through the surveys.

2. *Interpretive:* Analyzing the context and the survey data collected in an attempt to locate the "logjams" in ecumenical reception, especially in priestly formation.

3. *Normative:* Drawing on existing guidelines and proposals (i.e., best practices) to clarify "what ought to be going on" in terms of ecumenical ministerial formation.

4. *Pragmatic:* Proposing, based on the above, a revised practice to enhance the ecumenical formation of Canadian Anglican clergy in the seminaries, theological colleges, and other emerging training models in which they are prepared for ministry.

Each of these four spiraling movements will be evident in the unfolding chapters of this study, although the order in which they are presented will deviate slightly from the progression Osmer describes.

Chapter 1 focusses on the theological concept of reception, which is at the heart of this study. It first defines and then explores the idea broadly before focussing on how ecumenical scholars have applied the concept in a particular way in the pursuit of visible Christian unity, including understanding ecumenical formation as a means of ecumenical reception. It notes that the ecumenical formation of clergy is especially key in this process, the specifics of which are taken up in the following chapter.

Ecumenical theological education is the focus of the second chapter. Its roots are traced to a seminal moment in the life of the modern ecumenical movement, and the manner in which it developed thereafter, including

---

16. Swinton and Mowat, *Practical Theology*, 27.
17. Osmer, *Practical Theology*, 12.

Introduction

among Roman Catholics and Anglicans. Various models of ecumenical theological education will be explored, particularly those in Canada, and principles of ecumenical theological education will be named. Some of the desired practical outcomes of such an ecumenical formation will be examined through a review of three texts which promote the implementation of concrete and local expressions of ecumenical engagement. These provide the normative movement of the hermeneutical spiral.

The interdisciplinary dimension characteristic of practical theology is drawn out in chapter 3, which engages with the field of pedagogy in exploring transformative learning theory. With its genesis in the realm of adult education, transformative learning's potential application to a holistic form of ecumenical ministerial formation is evaluated. The all-encompassing ecumenical learning approach of the Ecumenical Institute at Bossey, Switzerland, is examined through the lens of transformative learning, and we will ask what specific attributes of this method might be transferable to other forms of ecumenical ministerial formation.

Chapter 4 describes in more detail the methods employed in the survey of Canadian Anglican theological colleges and seminaries and of the clergy. The results of the survey are presented and analyzed, satisfying the descriptive-empirical and interpretive movements of the hermeneutical spiral. They suggest a gap between what ought to be occurring in terms of local ecumenical engagement—as articulated by my church and by the relevant literature reviewed in chapter 2—and what is actually happening on the ground in congregational ministry.

The fifth chapter seeks to address this apparent gap through the proposal of a revised practice of ecumenical ministerial formation for those preparing for ordination in the Anglican Church of Canada. This is a pragmatic task, both in the sense of Osmer's use of the term to describe the final movement of the hermeneutical spiral, but also in that the proposed revised practice seeks to consider the realities and limitations currently faced by my denomination's institutions of ministerial formation and by their students.

This study concludes with some final reflections on the limitations of this research, including absent voices and paths not pursued, and some postulations about future directions for ecumenical ministerial formation in and beyond my church.

The ultimate goal of this research is to help shape future models of Anglican theological formation in Canada, especially that of the clergy, so that all the baptized of the Anglican Church of Canada can more fully live into our collective commitment to "walk the way of ecumenism."[18] Although this research approaches this problem through the specific lens of Canadian Anglicanism, my hope is that some of its content and findings might resonate with those in other contexts and Christian traditions who also desire their churches to be active and visible signs of reconciliation and transformation in a world in desperate need of both.

---

18. General Synod, "Towards a Renewed Ecumenical Strategy."

1

Reception

IF REGARDED FROM NOTHING other than a documentary standpoint, the last half-century of ecumenical conversations has been extraordinarily fruitful. Five tomes of ecumenical accords at the international level, collectively entitled *Growth in Agreement*, testify to just that: the ever-expanding degree of theological concordance reached among the largest and oldest of the separated churches in such once-divisive areas as Christology, pneumatology, salvation, sacraments, ministry, and authority. While marveling at the sheer volume of ecumenical agreements produced by bilateral and multilateral dialogues since the 1960s, the compilers of these anthologies of accords also acknowledge that in many cases these agreed statements risk having little life beyond the pages on which they are printed: "[I]f we do not want simply to mark time," they warn, "our primary task in the years to come must indeed be the implementation of fellowship on the basis of the consensus reached."[1]

Many other prominent voices in the ecumenical movement have suggested that theological ecumenism of the kind expressed in the work of bilateral dialogues like the Anglican-Roman Catholic International Commission (ARCIC) and multilateral roundtables like the Faith and Order Commission of the World Council of Churches has reached at least a temporary limit in its usefulness, given "the apparent inability of the sponsoring churches to build and move forward on the basis of what the dialogues have accomplished."[2] William Rusch has said that what is needed is not for

1. Meyer and Vischer, *Growth in Agreement I*, 8.
2. Rausch, "Reception Past and Present," 497.

dialogues to produce more solutions to the problem of Christian division, but rather "to have the solutions that have been found become decisive in the churches."[3] Even as far back as the 1970s, which some today would still consider ecumenism's heyday, Jürgen Moltmann lamented that, "At the present time, ecumenical theology seems to me to have developed to a point from which it can make no further headway unless there are changes in the churches's praxis."[4] Thirty-five years later a worldwide gathering in Assisi, Italy, sought to address the very same quandary, namely that formal ecumenical dialogue "has come to seem productive at the highest levels among churches yet less than effectual as an influence both on pastoral practice and in the lives of people within churches."[5]

What each of these observers of the ecumenical landscape is pointing to is the issue of reception. Whether a convergence statement on baptism or a theological agreement on ministry, to be truly effective the good in question needs to come into the possession of its intended recipient in such a way that it is translated into something tangible, useful, and effective. It needs to be received.

This chapter will conduct a brief survey of the theological concept of reception. I will concentrate on its ecumenical application and focus further still on what a number of writers on the topic have regarded as its spiritual dimension, and discuss some of the implications of such an understanding, particularly with respect to the formation of those preparing for ordained ministry. In doing so I will highlight the inextricable connection between ecumenical reception and ecumenical formation.

Defining 'Reception' in Its Different Forms

William Rusch has wryly observed that, "Everyone knows what reception is until someone is called upon to furnish a short and specific definition."[6] At the risk of validating his claim, I will venture to offer a definition of reception. I will actually present three, ranging from general to very specific. The task of defining this term has been made less onerous by the considerable literature devoted to the topic, especially among ecumenists, over the past four decades.

3. Rusch, *Ecumenical Reception*, 78.
4. Moltmann, "What Kind of Unity," 39.
5. Hughson, "Beyond Ecumenical Dialogue," 28.
6. Rusch, *Ecumenical Reception*, 136.

Reception

In its broadest sense, reception is "a process by which some material or spiritual good of one part comes into the possession of another."[7] The term was first used this way in the seventeenth century to demonstrate the manner in which Roman law had been appropriated by the German legal system. It has also been enlisted by the field of literary studies to describe the process that takes place between a text and its reader.[8]

Despite the term's general applicability, however, reception as a concept has found its most significant traction within ecclesiastical circles, particularly during the past forty years. Examples of reception can be drawn from throughout the church's history (as we shall see), and from the scriptures themselves. The apostle Paul reminds the Christians at Corinth that they have "received" the gospel he preached (1 Cor 15:1); Jesus describes the manner in which people "receive" (or not) the word in the parable of the sower (Matt 13:1–9; Mark 4:1–9; Luke 8:4–8); and the prologue of John's gospel describes how Christ "came unto his own, and his own received him not" (John 1:11). It was the convening of the Second Vatican Council that prompted the first really significant reflection on reception as an ecclesiological phenomenon: "Vatican II raised serious questions—and not just for the Roman Catholic Church—about the conciliar nature of the church, the teaching authority of the church, and how conciliar and other teachings were to be received into and made part of the life of the church."[9]

Among the first to attempt answers at those questions was Yves Congar, whose sweeping 1972 essay on reception was an original and systematic treatment of the concept from historical, theological, and ecclesiological perspectives. The definition of ecclesiastical reception he offered in that article remains a touchstone for any discussion of the topic: "By 'reception' we mean here the process by which an ecclesial body truly makes its own a definition that comes from elsewhere, and in doing so recognizing a rule that suits its life."[10]

Vatican II being the catalyst for Congar's reflections, his examples focused on the process by which the local churches made the decisions of the conciliar bodies their own. This process could be said to include two essential movements. To be truly effective, reception of something like a dogmatic definition would require both "explicit decisions" made by a juridical

---

7. Kilmartin, "Reception in History," 36.
8. Rusch, *Ecumenical Reception*, 2–3.
9. Rusch, *Ecumenical Reception*, 35.
10. Congar, "La réception," 370. Translated by author.

authority (such as an ecumenical council), but also a "wider and more complex" process of reception among the actual faithful of the church.[11] Approbation by church authorities alone is insufficient for reception to be authentic. For the "spiritual good" to be considered well and truly received, it required the church in its most local expressions to take possession. In the early church this was most frequently expressed through the incorporation of the received spiritual good (a creedal statement, for example) into the liturgical life of the local churches, thus eliciting what the Anglican-Roman Catholic International Commission has described as "the 'Amen' of the whole Church."[12]

Such a process in the early church was facilitated by the relative absence of formal divisions. Though culturally, linguistically, and geographically diverse, the churches of first few centuries of the Common Era were in large part churches in full communion with each other, and operated on the premise that "each church is truly church and so can speak to the other churches since all live from the same Spirit who guides the decisions."[13] This recognition of the other churches's ecclesiality facilitated the mutual exchange of doctrines, structures, and liturgies, issuing not just from recognized ecumenical councils but also particular churches.

Such widespread mutual recognition is not the reality of the church today. However, it was not long before ecumenists saw the manner in which the same questions that Congar was asking about reception within his own communion could be applied more widely to the reality confronting the divided churches in their quest for reconciliation and a more visible unity. As a result, a definition of reception particular to the ecumenical reality was needed, as opposed to the classical understanding of the term.

Thomas Rausch has furnished such a definition, describing *ecumenical* reception as "the acceptance by one church of a theological consensus arrived at with another church, and ultimately the recognition of the other church's faith and ecclesial life as authentically Christian."[14] Or, put another way, it is when "one finds true church authentically in the other."[15] It is this form of reception on which we will now concentrate, by examining the

---

11. Congar, "La réception," 373–74.
12. ARCIC II, *Gift of Authority*, 23.
13. Kilmartin, "Reception in History," 48.
14. Rausch, "Reception Past and Present," 497.
15. Budde, "Vocation for Unity," 99.

stages of the process, some examples of ecumenical reception, and the implications for the churches of the meaning of ecumenical reception.

The Process of Ecumenical Reception

As noted above, Congar's study of classical reception suggested a twofold process: approbation by an official juridical authority (such as a council), followed by a wider and more informal process of acceptance and integration by the local expressions of the church. When applied to the ecumenical context, other stages in this sequence can be identified. Günther Gassman, the late German Lutheran ecumenist and one-time director of the World Council of Churches's Commission on Faith and Order, suggests a threefold process in which the very first step—preceding any kind of official reception—is "'informal' reception."[16] This idea is reflected in the final report of the Lambeth Commission on Communion (better known as *The Windsor Report*), which was charged with addressing tensions emerging in the Anglican Communion in the late 1990s and early 2000s around divergent understandings of human sexuality. The commission's report dedicated a small section to reception, in which it articulated a three-step process similar to Gassman's:

1. theological debate and discussion;
2. formal action;
3. increased consultation to see whether the formal action is received—or, as the report puts it, whether it "settles down and makes itself at home."[17]

William Rusch goes further still in his deep reflections on the process of ecumenical reception, in which one can detect no fewer than five stages:

1. *Coexistence:* "When a particular church begins to perceive and to acknowledge that it is neither the sole bearer of Christian truth nor the sole witness to Christian faith";
2. *Cooperation:* When churches "recognize each other as churches to the extent that they are prepared to undertake certain tasks together, typically in such areas as community service and around issues concerning social justice";

16. Gassman, "From Reception to Unity," 118.
17. Anglican Communion, *Windsor Report*, 33.

3. *Dialogue:* When churches enter, in a formal way, into conversations aimed at "identifying specific obstacles to greater unity and understanding," and report back to their sponsoring churches on the progress made in surmounting those obstacles;

4. *Translation:* Rendering the theological agreements achieved by a dialogue "into practice in the living fellowship of the churches that have been represented in the dialogue";

5. *Response:* This represents "the first official word from a church about an ecumenical document," which "serves as a good indicator of how the process is going to proceed."[18]

Perhaps the most notable aspect of Rusch's working out of the process of ecumenical reception is his acknowledgement of that all-important initial step, what he describes as "coexistence." The mere act of one church's self-understanding developing to such a point that it sees value in entering into some kind of conversation or relationship—however initially tentative or informal—is no small move. It is the very considerable step the Catholic Church first took at the Second Vatican Council with its acknowledgement that "many elements of sanctification and of truth are found outside of its visible structure."[19] Jean-Marie Tillard observed that such a step already represents a limited degree of ecclesial recognition.[20] William Henn develops this further still when he notes that "the very fact of entering into dialogue, even prior to the production of any agreed statement, is already an act of reception, recognizing the other community as a sister to one's own community with whom, according to the will of Christ, one should be in full communion."[21]

Regardless of how many steps overall are enumerated in the process of ecumenical reception, two fundamental stages are unavoidable: the official approval of an agreed statement by the appropriate authorized bodies of the participating churches, and the wider reception of the implications of these agreed statements by the broad membership of the churches involved. As the ecumenical movement has amply witnessed in the past forty years, accomplishment of the first step is no guarantee of the second, and yet the second has no possibility of happening without that first official step. As I

---

18. Rusch, *Ecumenical Reception*, 72–75.
19. *Lumen Gentium*, §8
20. Tillard, "Fondements ecclésiologiques," 37.
21. Henn, "Reflections," 81.

will attempt to demonstrate, both of these fundamental stages of ecumenical reception have their own challenges.

Ecumenical Reception at a Juridical Level

The ecclesiological and structural diversity that the separated churches are seeking to reconcile is, in some cases, one of the very stumbling blocks in their ability to formally receive ecumenical agreements. Thomas Ryan summarizes the quandary well:

> The so-called "high churches" have no canonical compass for dealing with doctrinal materials admittedly co-authored by theologians representing other communions that are still officially condemned as either heretical or schismatic; and the so called "low-church" communions have no magisterial apparatus for determining what is or what is not the authentic faith of the Church, nor an authority of oversight to make such official declarations with binding authority for the beliefs of the faithful.[22]

Ryan was reflecting particularly on the challenges surrounding the reception process of *Baptism, Eucharist, and Ministry*, which as a document of the World Council of Churches invited hundreds of different churches with every ecclesial structure imaginable "to prepare an official response to this text at the highest appropriate level of authority."[23] However, even churches with a relatively recent common heritage have difficulty receiving bilateral ecumenically agreed statements at this formal level. As an example, an appendix to the Anglican-Roman Catholic International Commission's 1973 agreed statement on ministry goes to some lengths to stipulate that the document "is at present no more than a joint statement of the commission," adding, "It is not a declaration by the Roman Catholic Church or by the Anglican Communion. It does not authorize any change in existing ecclesiastical discipline."[24] To this day none of ARCIC's ten agreed statements has received the formal sanction of the Vatican. On the Anglican side, the Inter-Anglican Standing Commission on Ecumenical Relations (IASCER) noted in its final report in 2009 the unsatisfactorily piecemeal manner in which the Anglican Communion had been handling international-level

---

22. Ryan, "Reception," 31.
23. *Baptism, Eucharist and Ministry*, viii.
24. ARCIC I, "Status of the Document."

ecumenical agreements for most of its existence: "In practice, it has often been the case that whichever conciliar Instrument is meeting next is the one that takes note of ecumenical matters and/or sends out ecumenical texts."[25] The Lambeth Conference of bishops variously "recognizes," "welcomes," and "commends" much of ARCIC's work, but this body lacks the ability to formally receive or enact it. IASCER noted that the other three so-called Instruments of Communion—the Primates's Meeting, the Anglican Consultative Council, and the Archbishop of Canterbury—were also each in their own way individually inadequate to the task of receiving and implementing the increasingly voluminous and specialized output of the ecumenical dialogues of which the Anglican Communion was a part.[26] It was only in 2019 that the Anglican Consultative Council created a dedicated mechanism by which the Anglican Communion could officially receive the results of an ecumenical dialogue as "as consonant with the faith of the church as Anglicans have received it"[27]—five decades after the first international ecumenical agreed statement involving the Anglican Communion was issued.

Successful examples of the formal reception of ecumenical agreements are more easily found between Anglicans and Lutherans. There has been a small but steady proliferation of intercommunion or full communion agreements between these two traditions in the past twenty years. The relative success of the official adoption of these ecumenical agreed statements could be attributed in part to the fact that, unlike ARCIC, they have all been negotiated regionally. Lutheran and Anglican polity both place an important locus of their juridical authority in national or regional churches, and so establishing a full communion agreement between, for example, Anglicans and Lutherans in Canada was a more manageable task than attempting to receive agreed statements with communion-wide scope, like ARCIC.[28] At a formal level, enabling the full communion agreement

---

25. Rowland-Jones, *Vision Before Us*, 137.
26. Rowland-Jones, *Vision Before Us*, 138–39.
27. Anglican Consultative Council 17, resolution B17:04.
28. That is not to say the negotiating of ecumenical agreed statements at the regional level is not without its own problems. As more Anglican and Lutheran regional churches enter full communion relationships with each other, there has emerged the question of the degree to which these relationships are "transitive" to other parts of the world, where other similar agreements exist. For example, is a Swedish Lutheran in full communion with a Canadian Anglican because the Church of Sweden is in full communion with the Church of England, which is in full communion with the Anglican Church of Canada,

Reception

between these two churches required the approval of a sufficient majority of members of the General Synod of the Anglican Church of Canada and of the delegates to the National Convention of the Evangelical Lutheran Church in Canada, both of which were attained in 2001, albeit after years of official dialogue between the two churches.

Reception: 'No Mere Legal Category'

Taken on its own, the preceding description risks drawing a caricature of ecumenical reception as a theological and legislative process that is chiefly the business of bureaucratically mandated theologians, who negotiate the relevant esoteric points of theology, and of pedantic canonists, who sort out the necessary technical details to make the new ecclesial relationship regulatorily sound. There is necessarily a legislative and administrative dimension to ecumenical reception; someone has to work out the modalities of how the implications of such accords are to be lived out. If agreements between churches are to find concrete expression in the lives of the churches, they must be formally received by the authoritative bodies that order the lives of those churches, be they councils, conventions, presbyteries, or consistories. But this is only one part—perhaps even the smallest part—of the process of ecumenical reception. Those who have written at length about ecumenical reception go to some pains to stress this point. "Reception is not a dry practical idea," insists Orthodox theologian John Zizioulas.[29] Cardinal Johannes Willebrands, the one-time president of the Pontifical Council for Promoting Christian Unity, was similarly adamant: "Reception cannot and must not be understood as a purely technical or instrumental concept."[30] It is "no mere legal category," Rusch says. Rather

---

which is in full communion with the Evangelical Lutheran Church in Canada, which is also in full communion with the Church of Sweden? One focused attempt to resolve this question of ecclesial transitivity is a decision by all four Anglican and Lutheran full communion partners in North America to simply declare themselves in full communion with each other, by virtue of existing full communion agreements. So, for instance, the Anglican Church of Canada has declared itself in full communion with the Evangelical Lutheran Church in America (ELCA) because the ELCA is already in full communion with the Evangelical Lutheran Church in Canada and the Episcopal Church, both of which are already full communion partners of the Anglican Church of Canada.

29. Zizioulas, "Theological Problem," 4.
30. Willebrands, "Ecumenical Dialogue," 5.

it is "constitutive of the life of the church."[31] The process by which these theologically agreed statements become truly operative in the lives of the churches is itself theological.

Reception—whether speaking of the classical or the ecumenical kind—is a spiritual process, in the proper sense. That is to say it is a process inspired and guided by the Holy Spirit. Orthodox writers on reception, such as Nikos Nissiotis, are particularly insistent on this point: "The act of reception is the operation of the Holy Spirit communicating, in full freedom, the grace given by Christ to all persons who he wants to save, on the basis of their free decision."[32] He points to the account of council at Jerusalem in Acts 15, where the disciples validated Paul and Barnabas's new policy on the acceptance of non-Jewish believers, having concluded that "it has seemed good to the Holy Spirit and to us" to receive this new spiritual good (Acts 15:28). As noted above, it was on this pneumatological premise that the early churches received the decisions of the ecumenical councils: "[T]hese cases of reception of conciliar decisions by the church were neither in fact, nor understood by the churches to be, accomplished by a mere juridical act of acceptance by church officials; rather the juridical act was viewed as initiating a spiritual process of reception by the whole community."[33]

Examples of Non-Reception

Yet it is at this very point at which the process of reception can stall. Even if an ecumenical agreed statement is navigated through to official approbation by the respective church authorities, there is no guarantee of the second stage or reception—Congar's "wider and more complex" stage—happening in the wider church. Two ecumenical examples, one from the medieval church and another more recent, can illustrate this.

The Council of Florence (1431–1449) was possibly the most representative ecumenical council in Christian history and succeeded in producing a near-unanimous agreement on restoring to full communion the churches of the east and west after a five-century-old schism. All but one of the thirty-four Orthodox prelates present at the council signed the act of reunion with Rome. Yet as the Orthodox hierarchs returned to their home countries

---

31. Rusch, *Ecumenical Reception*, 7.
32. Nissiotis, "Meaning of Reception," 151.
33. Kilmartin, "Reception in History," 38.

Reception

and churches with news of their newly achieved reconciliation with Rome, they discovered in many cases that political and popular opinion were squarely against them. Not having prepared any kind of groundwork for such a controversial agreement within their local contexts, the results were predictable. Only days after reading aloud the Act of Union during the Divine Liturgy in Moscow's cathedral, the city's metropolitan archbishop was declared a heretic. Under threat of arrest and death, he fled (perhaps fittingly) to Rome. Bishops from many other parts of the Orthodox world recanted or were deposed.[34]

Rome's more recent efforts to heal another five hundred year old schism provides the second example. Signed jointly in 1999 by the Roman Catholic Church and the Lutheran World Federation, the Joint Declaration on the Doctrine of Justification (JDDJ) affirms that both communions "are now able to articulate a common understanding of our justification by God's grace through faith in Jesus Christ."[35] The defining theological point of contention of the Reformation had been resolved through the dialogical method of differentiated consensus—in effect, acknowledging there is more than one way to legitimately articulate the meaning of something in such a way that it need not be a cause of division. More aware of the challenges of reception than those gathered in council in Florence five hundred years before, the framers of the Catholic-Lutheran agreement recognized that "our consensus in basic truths on the doctrine of justification must come to influence the life and teaching of our churches."[36] Since Catholics and Lutherans promulgated the JDDJ in 1999, three other Christian world communions have also become signatories: the World Methodist Council (2006), the Anglican Communion (2016), and the World Communion of Reformed Churches (2017). Rusch has ruefully observed that notwithstanding the theological breakthrough the JDDJ represents, "the full import of the Joint Declaration seems lost on many."[37] At the same time, an event such as Pope Francis's very public participation in the commemorations of the Protestant Reformation in 2017 would not likely have been possible without the JDDJ and the "spiritual consensus and common witness in the service of the gospel" to which it points.[38]

---

34. Alfeyev, "Reception of Ecumenical Councils," 422.
35. JDDJ, §5.
36. JDDJ, §43.
37. Rusch, *Ecumenical Reception*, 104.
38. LWF and PCPCU, "Joint Statement."

Though no bishops, neither Lutheran nor Catholic, were run out of town as a result of their support of the Joint Declaration, the quiet indifference with which this landmark ecumenical agreement was received by the faithful of their communions speaks as loudly as the violent opposition of Orthodox Muscovites to the Council of Florence. Both represent examples of theologically sound ecumenical agreements that received the approbation of the respective churches's highest authorities, but failed to be received by the wider church in any meaningful way. If not outright examples of non-reception, they could perhaps be more optimistically termed examples of "semi-reception."

They both also point to the non-theological factors (or, as Meyer and Vischer prefer, "non-doctrinal factors"[39]) that can come into play in the reception process. It was, in significant part, the political intervention of the Grand Prince of Moscow that scuttled the Russian church's reunion with Rome in the fifteenth century. For Catholics and Lutherans (especially in Germany, the tumultuous cradle of Luther's reforms), centuries of lingering prejudices have diminished the reconciling effect the Joint Declaration might otherwise have had at the local church level. Meyer and Vischer observe that the impact of such political, historical, cultural, and psychological factors on ecumenical reception are usually easy to identify and analyze, but "how do we set about overcoming them when they have a divisive effect and hinder the reception of the agreements? This is another problem to which there is no quick answer."[40]

A Process Including the 'Entire People of God'

The churches can nevertheless draw lessons from the experiences of the Council of Florence and the Joint Declaration on the Doctrine of Justification. The only way to navigate—or altogether remove—obstacles of any kind to ecumenical reception is to take more seriously the essential role of the "entire people of God" in the process.[41] Churches engaged in ecumenical dialogue in many ways still behave in a manner that concentrates energy and resources on national- or international-level conversations without simultaneously preparing the ground regionally and locally for the fruits of those dialogues to be received. Nissiotis describes this phenomenon from

---

39. Meyer and Vischer, *Growth in Agreement I*, 9.
40. Meyer and Vischer, *Growth in Agreement I*, 9.
41. Willebrands, "Ecumenical Dialogue," 5.

Reception

the perspective of the Orthodox Church, but his observations can be applied more broadly: "The ecumenical dialogues, and even more the ecumenical fellowship, are restricted within hierarchical structures affecting only a small circle of specialists, or specially interested people, who have no access to the great masses of the Orthodox, especially in the ancient Orthodox mother churches of the east."[42]

Another Orthodox ecumenist, Alexandros Papadreos, characterizes this as "'bureautheology' (. . .), which in the long run is doomed to failure."[43] He suggests that even the most well-crafted ecumenical agreement is for naught without the cultivation of an ecumenical consciousness and desire throughout the church in all its expressions:

> Even if such a universal consensus were to be achieved at the highest level of authority competent here, it would have a real chance only if it were to fill the heart and conscience of the shepherds and the faithful with the assurance that the doctrinal differences of a kind which were fundamental and strong enough to separate us from the love of Christ and from communion with him and with one another no longer existed. The only way to prepare a consensus of this kind and to make the way for such an assurance is for synods, church authorities, congregations, theological schools, church mass media, our Christian education and our daily dealings with human beings who differ from us in faith and in thought to be filled and directed by the Spirit and (. . .) by the eucharistic experience of God, of the fellow human being, and of the world.[44]

What Papadreos envisions is an entirely holistic approach to ecumenical reception, in which all of the various constituencies of the church, acutely aware of the scandal of Christian division, seek its reconciliation. Both he and Nissiotis consider this a particular challenge within Orthodoxy, but ecumenists of other traditions also see the danger in making too many assumptions about the degree of knowledge or commitment to ecumenism among the faithful of their churches. Only twenty years after the Second Vatican Council, Tillard observed:

> Many Roman Catholics—laypeople, but also newly ordained priests and even certain bishops who did not experience the Second Vatican Council—have difficulty comprehending what we are

---

42. Nissiotis, "Meaning of Reception," 163.
43. Quoted by Ryan, "Reception," 31.
44. Quoted by Nissiotis, "Meaning of Reception," 163.

trying to explain. For them, unity means the "return" of others to the Catholic Church, which, gathered around the Bishop of Rome, is "the one true Church."[45]

Around the same time, Willebrands sounded the same caution:

> It is dangerously easy to take it for granted that everyone nowadays has already imbibed the ecumenical spirit of Vatican II. Yet the very fact that we are now celebrating the twentieth anniversary of the council should remind us that today's young priests and teachers, today's young parents, were little children at the time of the council and could not share in its experience in the way their elders did.[46]

How much more is this the case more than fifty years after the promulgation of the council's Decree on Ecumenism? There is, I believe, a similar risk in making assumptions by the degree to which a deep and lasting ecumenical spirit has been cultivated among those of other Christian traditions, including Canada's Anglicans.

The late Irish ecumenist Gerard Mannion also understood the uphill battle that ecumenical reception faces if the everyday faithful are not somehow included in the process. Drawing from the realm of international affairs, Mannion adapted a so-called "Tracks of Diplomacy Framework" to contemporary divided Christianity. In the diplomatic world "track 1" involves official voices like a sovereign state's foreign office personnel; in the ecumenical movement these official voices are members of theological dialogues formally representing their churches. Both types engage in protracted talks aimed at achieving some form of binding consensus. "Track 2" in the world of diplomacy and ecumenism both involves "non-official and grassroots voices and practitioners" helping create the conditions for the consensus to be successfully received locally.[47]

A political application of this framework was the 1998 Good Friday Agreement, which ended decades of sectarian violence in Northern Ireland. Track 1 of this peace accord involved formal negotiations between the British and Irish governments and other political parties or groupings, resulting in a unanimous negotiated settlement. However,

> any official outcome would have been fruitless unless received into an already changing set of conditions that had been emerging

---

45. Tillard, "Fondements ecclésiologiques," 30. Translated by author.
46. Willebrands, "Ecumenical Dialogue," 7.
47. Mannion, "Assisi 2012," 148–49.

Reception

from grassroots developments. A successful outcome depended on an accompanying independent parallel track 2 in local, unofficial initiatives and on an allying of personal, familial, and neighborhood interests toward a peaceful Northern Ireland. Art, poetry, music, and literature played indispensable roles.[48]

The two tracks are intended to run parallel and rely on each other for reception to be successfully achieved: "A track 2 in diplomacy or ecumenism generates conditions for the possibility of receiving an accord reached on track 1."[49] An ecumenical example of this framework not being applied would be the ill-fated Council of Florence, which operated exclusively on that first track, ignoring to its peril the actual local context onto which the officially negotiated agreement would be applied. This two-track understanding of reflection provides another helpful way of understanding the process of reception as one that involves both a hierarchical or juridical aspect and a local or spiritual one.

Ecumenical Spirituality and Ecumenical Formation

How then to inspire this ecumenical spirit and desire for communion? How do we who are firmly convinced that the full communion of the churches is a divine imperative inculcate this conviction in others? This will be accomplished through nothing less than what Willebrands describes as "an all-embracing ecumenical spirituality and ecumenical formation."[50] He and many others have suggested that long before divided churches are in relationships of full communion, their individual members and communities can engage in a large number and variety of types of spiritual ecumenism. Entire guides and manuals exist detailing how Christians of different traditions can draw from the fundamental level of agreement their churches already share and engage in forms of common worship, mission, evangelism, public witness, and education. Such activities are not to be simply seen as some kind of stopgap activity in which divided Christians can engage until their churches are fully reconciled. Rather these joint initiatives, made possible by the real if imperfect communion divided Christians already share, can be the fertile soil into which later theological agreed statements and declarations can be planted, thus ensuring a better chance of their taking

48. Hughson, "Beyond Ecumenical Dialogue," 25.
49. Hughson, "Beyond Ecumenical Dialogue," 25–26.
50. Hughson, "Beyond Ecumenical Dialogue," 25–26.

root and growing—and even provide the very impetus for those theological agreements to be created:

> Through this ecumenical practice of the faith it may be expected that the churches will experience their profound unity in Christ—and so their separation—as something which deeply affects the life of faith in all churches. It is the common practice of faith which both enables the churches to recognize one another as "sister" churches and, at the same time, fosters the sense of incompleteness of the life of faith as long as the separation persists.[51]

Notwithstanding a high level of engagement and initiative among many of the laity in the churches, to truly flourish, the kind of ecumenical spirituality envisioned here will need to have the committed involvement of the churches's leadership, especially locally. In churches with theologically trained ordained leaders, the need for ecumenical formation becomes even more key. In the Roman Catholic Church, for example, official guidelines exist for the ecumenical formation of priests. However, the extent to which these guidelines are applied—or even known—is inconsistent. The late Canadian Catholic theological educator Margaret O'Gara has argued that if those formational guidelines were applied to the full extent envisioned, the result would be nothing less than transformational not only for the individual priests, but for the churches they will serve: "Behind in the innocuous term 'ecumenical formation' stands the reality of conversion and the change that conversion demands. The effects of such ecumenical formation would be a profound transformation of the Roman Catholic Church."[52] Once again, these observations can be applied widely. If all of the churches's theologically trained leaders had a thorough and authentic ecumenical formation, how might that transform the current ecclesial landscape?

Conversion or 'Cheap Unity'?

O'Gara compellingly suggests that a seminarian's ecumenical formation should result in nothing less than a conversion experience—a profound, life-changing commitment to a new course of action. Authentic ecumenical reception demands nothing less of the churches. In the contemporary context of divided Christianity, the fullest form of ecumenical reception

---

51. Kilmartin, "Reception in History," 53–54.
52. O'Gara, "Formation and Transformation," 26.

means recognition: "We must remember that reception is not a matter of texts alone, but of churches and people. In the very act of reacting to texts the churches enter a process of receiving each other as churches."[53] The natural conclusion of that process is full ecclesial recognition. Rusch states the ultimate goal most plainly:

> If divided churches are able to receive fully the positive conclusions of their ecumenical dialogues with other churches, then these churches should be able to recognize those other churches as fully Church. Therefore they should be able to enter into full communion with them.[54]

The risk of entering into a relationship of any kind is that one might be changed by the encounter. Relationships between churches are no different in this respect. Tillard insists that one church fully recognizing the ecclesiality of the other can result in nothing other than a change in the recognizing church, otherwise it is simply what he calls a "cheap unity": "It is certain that to enter into communion with another will require a change in our attitudes, a certain upheaval in our preconceived ideas, perhaps even a change in our pastoral practice. To accept to be in communion—that is to say, to 'receive' this or that community—is to accept to be disrupted."[55]

A church's ability and willingness to be "disrupted" by its ecumenical partner—and yet fully recognize them as Church—is a measure of the degree to which it has had its conversion experience. Thomas Ryan agrees: "Unlike the recipient of a material good, the recipient of a spiritual good must be changed; a new synthesis must take place which cannot be forced or made to happen quickly."[56]

Ecumenical reception can be neither compelled nor rushed. Like the kingdom of God, one here might easily fall into the trap of works righteousness, misunderstanding the church's unity as something we ourselves can build or make visible, rather than as something inherent we can at best help make less obscured. As for the length of the process of reception, Congar points out that even the doctrinal decisions of the First Council of Nicaea took more than fifty years to be fully received. Alfeyev notes that the Christological definitions of the Council of Chalcedon are still technically in the process of being received by some of the churches represented

---

53. Zizioulas, "Theological Problem," 6.
54. Rusch, *Ecumenical Reception*, 87.
55. Tillard, "Fondements ecclésiologiques," 34. Translated by author.
56. Ryan, "Reception," 29.

at that gathering—which concluded meeting one thousand five hundred years ago.[57] This provides some credence to Donna Geernaert's concluding remark when the Canadian Catholic ecumenist was invited to speak on ecumenical reception at a meeting of the Faith and Order Commission in 1996: "What may be most helpful in this context is prayer, patience, and a sense of humor."[58]

Ecumenical Formation as a Means of Ecumenical Reception

Yet even if God's kingdom—which Jesus Christ tells us is already in our midst, albeit in an obscured and imperfect form—cannot be forced or rushed, Christians are nevertheless called to seek to reveal it further here and now. So too with the visible unity of Christ's church. As we have seen, ecumenical reception is the process by which this ecclesial mutual recognition occurs. Up until now the primary means of effecting ecumenical reception between the churches has been through international-level dialogues negotiating agreements (Mannion's "track 1" ecumenism), which has effected much theologically rapprochement, but with relatively little impact on the more local expressions of the churches involved. Accomplishing this second movement ("track 2" ecumenism) requires ecumenically conscientious and committed ecumenical practitioners on the ground who have cultivated "a substratum of momentum, desire, hope, and commitment expressed in insights, local praxis, and creative art able to inspire and instruct track 1."[59]

These ecumenical practitioners in turn need to be cultivated to become, in effect, agents of ecumenical reception in their respective proper contexts, essentially "training clergy for ecumenical reception in the local church (. . .)."[60] In the same way that Mannion's two ecumenical tracks are interconnected and mutually reliant, so too are ecumenical reception and ecumenical formation. This has been especially stressed by the Joint Working Group between the Roman Catholic Church and the World Council of Churches (JWG), whose work we will see in more detail in the next chapter. The JWG had become so preoccupied with the issue—and evident lack—of ecumenical reception that not only did it dedicate an entire section of its

---

57. Alfeyev, "Reception of Ecumenical Councils," 421.
58. Geernaert, "Reception: A Canadian Perspective," 94.
59. Hughson, "Beyond Ecumenical Dialogue," 26.
60. Budde, "The Vocation for Unity," 98.

2013 final report to reception, but it also had that chapter produced as a separate publication, in the hope that "its separate appearance here may make this valuable study of this dynamic element in ecumenical understanding available to a broader audience."[61] That part of the report describes reception as "a key to ecumenical progress," and within it includes a separate section on ecumenical formation, which it in turns describes as "a key to ecumenical reception":

> Ecumenical formation is in itself a way of consolidating reception. As people listen to the history of the ecumenical movement and receive the fruits of ecumenical dialogue, they themselves are deepening their formation as disciples of Christ. The multiplex process of reception requires a process of education and formation which embraces both the intellectual and theological dimensions of being trained in ecumenical dialogue and the existential and spiritual dimensions of receiving and recognizing one another in the name of Christ. Ecumenical formation and reception, therefore, are intrinsically intertwined.[62]

The document goes on to identify theological education, and particularly the education of pastors, as a "crucial area" for ecumenical formation.[63] With this inextricable link between ecumenical reception and ecumenical formation in mind, we will now start to consider the ecumenical formation of prospective clergy in the Anglican Church of Canada, beginning with an exploration of some of the history, principles, and models of ecumenical theological education.

---

61. Joint Working Group, *Reception*, ix.
62. Joint Working Group, *Reception*, 56.
63. Joint Working Group, *Reception*, 56.

2

Ecumenical Theological Education

THE QUEST FOR THE visible unity of the church has, especially over the past century, become a particular preoccupation for Anglicans. One historian goes as far as to suggest that "an ecumenical vocation has become part of Anglican self-understanding."[1] If this is so, a significant part of this cultivation of ecumenical consciousness can be attributed to the theological education of recent generations of Anglican clergy, who themselves play a particular role of teaching and leadership in the church. The form and content of one's priestly formation fundamentally influences the form and content of one's priestly ministry, and potentially the life and work of the wider church, including its ecumenical dimension: "[T]heological education is the seedbed for the renewal of the churches, their ministries and mission, and their commitment to the church's unity in today's world."[2]

This chapter will explore in an initial way the ecumenical dimension of the theological education of Anglicans preparing for ordination, particularly in Canada. After defining some key terms, I will conduct a brief historical survey of such ecumenical formation, paying special attention to models and institutions that have emerged in this country. The principles that have undergirded these efforts will be examined, especially as they have been expressed by two entities which have dedicated extensive thought (separately and together) to the question: the World Council of Churches and the Roman Catholic Church. I will also look at emerging attempts by the Anglican Communion and the Anglican Church of Canada

1. Butler, "History of Anglicanism," 46.
2. Werner, "Ecumenical Formation," 108.

to give their own expression of principles of ecumenical theological formation. The content that might characterize a well-rounded ecumenical ministerial formation will be discussed, as will its objectives.

Defining Terms

Ecumenical ministerial formation is the preferred term for the kind of instruction for future clergy under discussion here. Each of this term's constituent words might in turn benefit from a brief definition of their own.

The need to define a term as basic to this discussion as *ecumenical* might at first seem unnecessary. However, over time the word taken on different meanings for different churches, groups, or individuals, such that "we can no longer take a common understanding of the ecumenical vocation for granted."[3] One ecumenical scholar has enumerated at least four different understandings of ecumenism used in current discourse, one of which conflates the otherwise distinct understandings of ecumenical and interreligious dialogue.[4] In 1997 the United Church of Canada officially adopted such an approach under the moniker of "whole world ecumenism," defined as a "broader ecumenism [that] is world-centered, placing emphasis on churches relating to the world beyond themselves, to persons involved in other religious traditions, ideologies, and secular agencies."[5]

This present discussion adopts what might be called a classical understanding of ecumenism as the ongoing effort by the separated Christian churches to "call one another to visible unity in one faith and in one eucharistic fellowship, expressed in worship and common life in Christ, through witness and service to the world, by which we advance towards that unity in order that the world may believe."[6]

Formation implies a more holistic approach than terms such as *learning*, *training*, or even *education*: "It refers to the whole process of equipping, raising awareness, shaping or transforming attitudes and values."[7] As we shall see, this multifaceted pedagogical approach is seen as key to elevating an individual's ecumenical consciousness and engagement, and developing their "ecumenical competence," defined as "the ability to appreciate and

---

3. Raiser, "Fifty Years," 447.
4. Weber, "Laboratory for Ecumenical Life," 436.
5. United Church of Canada, "Mending the World."
6. World Council of Churches, *Constitution and Rules*, §III.
7. Raiser, "Fifty Years," 440.

understand the otherness of different church traditions, not as a threat but as an enrichment."[8] The desired outcomes of such an ecumenical formation for a parish-based pastor will be named later. We will also discuss these potentially "transforming" effects of ecumenical formation by delving in a later chapter into the idea of transformative learning itself.

Finally, the particular kind of ecumenical formation that is the focus of this discussion is *ministerial*, that is "programs and institutions which on a more formal basis offer courses and training programs for future ordained church ministers to be fully theologically, liturgically, pastorally, and catechetically trained and equipped for their ministry."[9] Ecumenical formation is for the whole people of God, not only the ordained. It represents "an ongoing process of learning within the various local churches and world communions, aimed at informing at building people in the movement which—inspired by the Holy Spirit—seeks the visible unity of Christians."[10] However, even though all Christians ought to be formed ecumenically, the mandated teaching, pastoral, and leadership responsibilities of the clergy makes their participation in this process of "strategic importance"[11] since they play "a central role in animating such formation."[12]

The 1910 World Missionary Conference

The birthplace of the modern ecumenical movement is typically traced back to the 1910 meeting of the World Missionary Conference. About twelve hundred representatives of mostly Protestant and Anglican churches in Europe and North America gathered in Edinburgh, Scotland, in response to a growing recognition that denominational competitiveness in overseas missions was compromising all of the churches's missionary efforts by presenting a fractured Christian witness to the objects of their evangelization. This, along with dividing or duplicating resources in the missionary field, was described by one plain-speaking American delegate to the conference as "preposterous."[13]

---

8. Raiser, "Importance of the Ecumenical Vision," 81.
9. Werner, "Ecumenical Learning," 3.
10. Joint Working Group, *Seventh Report*, §9.
11. Joint Working Group, *Seventh Report*, §13.
12. PCPCU, *Ecumenical Dimension,* §A.[3].
13. World Missionary Conference, *Report of Commission V*, 180–81.

Ecumenical Theological Education

The separate manner in which the various churches and missionary societies prepared their personnel for their overseas work was singled out for criticism by the conference, which had an entire commission (on "the Training of Teachers") dedicated to an evaluation of the preparation of those serving in the mission field. It concluded that such training "cannot be adequately met by existing institutions, or by [missionary] societies separately," and went on to declare that "the time has fully come when the boards [of missionary societies] should cooperate in an advance step." The commission proposed that the churches and missionary societies eschew competition and instead work in "combination" and "cooperation" through "central missionary colleges" in which missionaries of different denominations would be trained together.[14]

Like the World Missionary Conference itself, the recommendation was a precursor and without precedent: "These plans were visionary and revolutionary in their understanding of Christian education and theological education in particular—an early foretaste of the concept of ecumenical theological education and ecumenical learning which was developed decades later."[15]

Exactly one decade later, Orthodox voices—which were not present at Edinburgh—made their own similar call. In 1920 the Ecumenical Patriarchate of Constantinople issued a groundbreaking encyclical that included several recommendations for the cultivation of "friendship and kindly disposition" among the divided churches, two of which specifically related to ministerial formation. One encouraged the development of "relationships between the theological schools and the professors of theology," and another suggested "exchanging students for further training between the seminaries of the different churches."[16]

World Council of Churches

As we shall see, efforts to put into practice a cooperative model of theological education of the kind the Edinburgh conference envisioned for missionary formation began in the decade immediately following 1910. However, it would be decades more before ecumenical education, especially for future church leaders, would begin to become a priority for the wider ecumenical movement.

14. World Missionary Conference, *Report of Commission V*, 180–81, 330.
15. Werner, "Theological Education," 92.
16. Ecumenical Patriarchate, "Unto the Churches of Christ Everywhere."

Formation for Transformation

The first and perhaps most radical foray into this was establishment of the Ecumenical Institute at Bossey, Switzerland. Since opening in a converted rural Genevan chateau in 1946 (two years before the creation of the World Council of Churches (WCC), which subsequently acquired ownership), the Ecumenical Institute has annually brought together laity and clergy from around the world and from most every Christian tradition for a fully residential program of ecumenical formation lasting anywhere between five to twelve months. The intensive program includes not only accredited academic studies in ecumenics, but less formal (and, as we shall see, no less formative) experiences of common prayer, shared meals, and co-ed living arrangements. This unique form of ecumenical education has earned Bossey a reputation as "a sort of laboratory where ecumenism is being lived."[17]

However indelible a mark a sojourn at Bossey might make on the ecumenical consciousness of its students, the number of people the institute could directly impact in this way was fewer than fifty each year. Those within the World Council of Churches deeply committed to the cause of ecumenism soon began to realize that most of them had first captured an ecumenical spirit through programs like those offered by Bossey or in other "training grounds" such as the World Student Christian Federation, and not from their local churches: "The implication of this was that ecumenical awareness would be available only to a very few people as such opportunities declined or became less attractive. The development of an ecumenical consciousness would remain the privilege of a few ecumenical insiders."[18]

It was this realization that in part prompted the WCC to broaden its engagement in ecumenical formation. The Theological Education Fund was established in 1958 as a way of financially supporting ministerial formation in so-called "younger churches" in the developing world. In 1977 the fund was folded into the structures of the WCC, which created an entire programmatic area dedicated to "ecumenical education." Later renamed "ecumenical formation," it remains one of the WCC's three main focuses of programmatic work, and to "nurture the growth of an ecumenical consciousness through processes of education" is a priority enshrined in the council's constitution.[19] We will see how the WCC's preoccupation with

---

17. Weber, "Laboratory for Ecumenical Life," 436.
18. Becker, "Ecumenical Formation," 183.
19. World Council of Churches, *Constitution and Rules*, §III.

ecumenical formation has resulted in some of the most developed thinking on this question.

Organizational Models of Ecumenical Theological Education

Even before the WCC came to understand ecumenical ministerial formation as key to securing the ecumenical movement's memory and future, individual churches and teaching institutions were already moving more closely together in the way the Edinburgh missionary conference envisioned.

This was especially the case in North America, although such cooperation was not necessarily intuitive. Even into the twentieth century, theological schools in Canada and the United States were practically all directly related to a particular church tradition or denomination, many of which had their roots in Europe. A striking illustration of a mother country's theological traditions looming large in its colonies was McGill University's Divinity Hall, completed on the downtown Montreal campus in 1931, which was decorated with the imposing portraits of "eleven British Christian notables—ten English and one Scottish."[20]

Nevertheless, whether inspired by an ecumenical vision or more pragmatic motives, institutions of ministerial formation began to seek ways to work cooperatively. Among the first moves in this rapprochement was the establishment in 1920 of the Conference of Theological Seminaries (CTS). Like the World Missionary Conference of a decade before, the CTS was heavily American and largely liberal Protestant. Even so, the schools that did participate in the organization "crossed a huge dividing (and sometimes battle) line in the nineteenth century: denominationalism."[21]

The kind of encounters between Christian traditions and denominational schools initially made possible by the CTS (and then by its successor bodies) opened the doors to unprecedented forms of ecumenical collaboration:

> By the middle of the twentieth century, an ecumenical orientation for theological education became conspicuous, as federative or cooperative clusters or consortia of schools of different denominational backgrounds were organized, and as denominational

---

20. Handy, "Trends," 190. Those portraits, all of them of men, hang to this day in what is now called the Birks Building, home to McGill's School of Religious Studies.

21. Aleshire, "Theological Education," 505.

theological schools merged their resources in forming new ecumenical institutions.[22]

Canada proved especially fertile ground for such experiments in ecumenical theological education. One historian has suggested this could be attributed to a number of factors particular to the Canadian context: too much geography, too many small institutions, not enough resources, and opportunities for partnerships provided by affiliation with universities.[23] Whatever the reasons, the twentieth century saw many Canadian institutions for ministerial formation forgo complete independence as stand-alone denominational schools to enter into various configurations of ecumenical partnership.

The earliest example of this emerged in Montreal, where in 1912 individual theological colleges preparing candidates for ministry in the Anglican, Congregationalist, Methodist, and Presbyterian churches established a formal agreement among themselves and with McGill University whereby students would together receive academic theological formation through the university's divinity (later religious studies) faculty (later school), while instruction of a more pastoral or professional nature would be offered by the individual denominational colleges. This model of denominational divinity schools "integral to a university" mirrors similar arrangements with American schools such as Harvard, Howard, Chicago, Vanderbilt, and Yale.[24] A century later, Anglican, Presbyterian, and United Church of Canada colleges maintain this relationship with McGill under the moniker of the Montreal School of Theology.

Still more daring experiments in ecumenical collaboration in theological education were to come. Partly in anticipation of an organic union between the Anglican Church of Canada and the United Church of Canada that was in the end never realized, the two denominations's divinity schools in Vancouver merged in 1971 into a single institution (into which a Presbyterian divinity school later joined). In the same year, on the opposite side of the country, long-separate Anglican, Roman Catholic, and United Church schools merged into the newly branded Atlantic School of Theology (AST) under a single board of governors, faculty, student body, and curriculum: "From its inception the school has been by design an integrated community,

---

22. Handy, "Trends," 202.
23. Handy, "Trends," 204.
24. Handy, "Trends," 203.

Ecumenical Theological Education

not a federation of institutions or programs. It has one ecumenical faculty and all students study in fully integrated courses."[25]

Still another model emerged around the same time among the constellation of church-sponsored colleges that had begun federating or otherwise affiliating with the secular University of Toronto in the late nineteenth century. Active collaboration among them began in the 1940s in the area of graduate studies. Continued cooperation led to the establishment in 1970 of the Toronto School of Theology (TST), a formal consortium of seven institutions representing the Anglican, Presbyterian, Roman Catholic, and United Church traditions. (Though not members of the consortium, Christian Reformed, Mennonite, and Lutheran institutions are also affiliated with the TST.) Students belong to one of the consortium's seven colleges, but have some freedom to take courses through any of the others, although as we shall see, the degree to which this freedom is exercised is relatively small.

Notable in the Halifax and Toronto models is the participation of Roman Catholic Church, a reality made possible by Catholicism's full entry into the ecumenical movement following the Second Vatican Council. At Ottawa's Saint Paul University, an Anglican studies program for the formation of clergy has been integrated into the school's pontifically chartered faculty of theology since 1981. Though formal Catholic commitment to these partnerships has been steadfast, few men actually training for priesthood receive the kind of ecumenical exposure these contexts would presumably provide, since most are sent to be formed in the almost exclusively Catholic surroundings of a major seminary. Still, relative to its pre-conciliar stance of stalwart non-participation in the ecumenical movement, Catholic engagement in theological education in Canada and the U.S. proved in many ways transformational:

> Prior to 1964 [the year Vatican II's Decree on Ecumenism was promulgated], the conversation among theological educators had been a Protestant conversation. After 1964, the conversation shifted, and the two dominant Christian communities in North America that had existed in isolation from one another were now in conversation, discovering both their unique practices and traditions, and the common concerns of running a theological school.[26]

This was reflected in the membership of the Association of the Theological Schools in the United States in Canada (ATS), the successor body of

25. Krieger, MacDermid, and Mabey, "Atlantic School of Theology," 34.
26. Aleshire, "Theological Education," 508.

Formation for Transformation

the Conference of Theological Seminaries, which became the principle accrediting body for North America's theological schools. Before 1964 there were no Roman Catholic institutions among its members. A decade later there were fifty-six. The membership of ATS continues to reflect the diverse ecclesial complexion of the continent, now counting among its more than two hundred and fifty member schools a number of Eastern Orthodox and historically African American institutions, and nearly one-hundred schools that could be classified as "Evangelical Protestant." That being said, membership in ATS does not imply a school is participating in some form of ecumenical consortium or that an institution is even inclined to work with institutions of other traditions.

For all the seeming progress made in ecumenical approaches to theological education over the past century, especially institutionally, there are also signs of retrenchment. Former WCC General Secretary Konrad Raiser has observed an overall weakening in the ecumenical dimension of theological education, such that "even formerly interdenominational theological schools or coalitions of different denominational theological institutions are being dissolved in favor of a renewed denominational orientation."[27] Even while seeking to continue work ecumenically, some churches are confronted by the challenge of internal divisions, which can have a direct impact on their schools of ministerial formation.[28] In the next section of this chapter, we will explore why ecumenists like Raiser see the maintenance—and deepening—of ecumenical collaboration in ministerial formation as essential not only for the sake of the church, but of the world.

Principles of Ecumenical Theological Education

This discussion up until now has been largely historical and structural, a brief survey of some of the different organizational models employed over time by schools of ministerial formation seeking to work together more closely.[29] But to what end, and by what means? This section will explore

27. Raiser, "Fifty Years," 448.

28. An example is Nashotah House, a seminary in the Anglo-Catholic tradition located in Wisconsin, which is currently experiencing the tensions of being an institution recognized and governed by members of both the Episcopal Church and the rival Anglican Church in North America.

29. These different organizational models could be said to mirror various different models of unity that have been operative at one point or another in the ecumenical movement. For example, VST and AST arguably reflect the organic union model, the

some of the principles of ecumenical ministerial formation that have been developed, sometimes out of the very experience of some of the joint educational ventures that have been highlighted. Special attention will be paid to the contributions of two institutions which have developed—both separately and together—the clearest articulation of what effective ecumenical ministerial formation ought to resemble: the World Council of Churches and the Roman Catholic Church. In so doing I will attempt to identify points of contact and demonstrate a shared understanding for a framework for ecumenical ministerial formation, at least around a few key concepts.

World Council of Churches

As noted above, ecumenical formation has for decades been a programmatic focus of the WCC, and is enshrined as a constitutional mandate. In 2012 the WCC's Central Committee reaffirmed that "ecumenical formation and theological education should receive a visible, distinct and strong role in the future working agenda and structure of the WCC (. . .)."[30] Space prohibits a fulsome survey of the evolution of the WCC's approach to ecumenical formation, which has included a preoccupation with such learning for laity and clergy both, as well as support of theological education among its member churches, particularly those in the Global South. Some of the most recent articulations of principles for ecumenical formation from the perspective of the WCC can be found in two sources, and these will be the ones from which I chiefly draw. One is "*Magna Charta* on Ecumenical Formation in Theological Education in the Twenty-First Century—Ten Key Convictions," a 2008 reference document of the WCC's program on ecumenical theological education.[31] The other emerged out of a series of structured "ecumenical conversations" on ecumenical formation at the tenth assembly of the WCC in Busan, South Korea, the salient points of which were subsequently published.[32]

Montreal School of Theology and Saint Paul University full communion, and TST reconciled diversity.

    30. World Council of Churches, "Ecumenical Covenant," §VII.

    31. Werner, "*Magna Charta*," 161–70.

    32. World Council of Churches, *Ecumenical Conversations*, 35–44.

Roman Catholic Church

It was the Second Vatican Council's Decree on Ecumenism, *Unitatis Redintegratio*, that thrust the Catholic Church into the modern ecumenical movement and articulated the principles guiding its participation in this collective effort for the "restoration of unity among all Christians."[33] The practical implications of these newly established Catholic ecumenical principles were spelled out soon after in the *Ecumenical Directory*, first issued in two parts in 1967 and 1970. In its current form, revised in 1993, the *Directory for the Application of Principles and Norms on Ecumenism* dedicates one of its five sections to "Ecumenical Formation in the Catholic Church."[34] The specific implications of Catholic ecumenical participation on the formation of clergy was elucidated further still in 1995 by the release of *The Ecumenical Dimension in the Formation of Those Engaged in Pastoral Work*. This "study document" acknowledges that one of the *Directory*'s principle concerns is "ecumenical formation in seminaries and theological faculties," and so concentrates on advising these teaching institutions on "providing an ecumenical dimension to the formation of those engaged in pastoral work" and "outlining the contents of a specialized course in ecumenism."[35] The *Directory* and the subsequent study text combined represent the clearest articulation of an official Catholic vision of ecumenical ministerial formation. Indeed, taken together the documents have been described as "the fullest explication of ecumenical education and formation by any church or Christian world communion."[36]

Joint Working Group

Given the attention the World Council of Churches and the Roman Catholic Church have each accorded the matter of ecumenical ministerial formation individually, it is unsurprising that it has been a recurring theme in their official bilateral conversations. Even before the Second Vatican Council had concluded, the Joint Working Group between the Roman Catholic Church and the World Council of Churches (JWG) was established with a mandate to "to examine possibilities in the field of dialogue and cooperation"

---

33. *Unitatis Redintegratio*, §1.
34. PCPCU, *Directory*, 37–55.
35. PCPCU, *Ecumenical Dimension*, Preface.
36. Joint Working Group, *Seventh Report*, §4.

between the two.[37] From its very first report in 1965, when "the training of clergy and laity with an ecumenical outlook" was identified as a "major issue" on its agenda, the JWG has paid special attention to the question of ecumenical ministerial formation; it is mentioned in all but one of the JWG's nine official reports. The issue is given a particularly fulsome treatment in the Joint Working Group's seventh (1998) and ninth (2013) reports, the former including an entire appendix dedicated to articulating principles of ecumenical formation and the latter building on this by reflecting on the link between ecumenical formation and ecumenical reception. Both will be important sources for this discussion.

The Joint Working Group conducted especially significant work on ecumenical formation in the late 1980s and early 1990s, producing a study document in 1993 (which became the aforementioned appendix in 1998) entitled *Ecumenical Formation: Ecumenical Reflections and Suggestions*. Invoking the ecumenical imperative drawn from Jesus' high priestly prayer—that his disciples "may all be one . . . so that the world may believe that you have sent me" (John 17:21)—the document describes ecumenical formation as "a matter of urgency because it is part of the struggle to overcome the divisions of Christians which are sinful and scandalous and challenge the credibility of the church and her mission."[38]

Some of the specific means of ecumenical formation recommended by the JWG document will be discussed later. However, in brief it advocates a holistic approach that includes not only the absorption of knowledge about the ecumenical movement—such as the study of ecumenical history and the documentary fruits of interchurch dialogues—but also "a certain bold openness to living ecumenically as well."[39] This involves the cultivation of an "ecumenical spirituality" that is rooted in "learning in community," which includes common prayer with Christians of other traditions and exposure to other churches's spiritual texts, prayers, and songs.[40]

Such a "wholehearted" approach to ecumenical formation creates the possibility for the "change of heart which is the very soul of the work

---

37. Joint Working Group, "First Official Report," 244. Though not a member church of the WCC, the Catholic Church works collaboratively with the council wherever possible, and the JWG helps coordinate these efforts. The Catholic Church is a full member of the Commission on Faith and Order, the WCC's official theological roundtable.

38. Joint Working Group, *Seventh Report*, §3.

39. Joint Working Group, *Seventh Report*, §12.

40. Joint Working Group, *Seventh Report*, §21, 15.

for restoring Christian unity."[41] One of the practical outcomes of such an ecumenical conversion would be "to eliminate polemic and to further mutual understanding, reconciliation and the healing of memories."[42] The document grounds this approach in the theology of *koinonia*, understanding the church as a reflection of the Trinity's "communion of rich diversity," which, though consisting of differentiated members, has nevertheless been created for unity.[43]

The document also suggests ecumenical formation address the matters of religious plurality and secularism, while noting that the different goals of interreligious dialogue and of ecumenism must be carefully distinguished. With a prescient cautious optimism—and without explicitly naming the internet, which in 1993 was still in relatively infancy—the text also names "mass communication" as a possible tool for "communicating the ecumenical spirit."[44]

It should be noted that a certain degree of Anglican influence and ethos can be assumed to be present in the recommendations of the Joint Working Group, including the *Ecumenical Formation* study document. Many provinces of the Anglican Communion—including the Anglican Church of Canada—are charter members of the World Council of Churches, and most iterations of the JWG have included Anglicans among the WCC's representation, including at least three Canadians: the Rev. Donald Anderson, Bishop David Hamid, and the Rev. Canon Dr. John Gibaut. So, while a multilateral work involving several ecclesial traditions, the JWG's recommendations on ecumenical formation can to some extent be understood to reflect an Anglican approach.

Anglican Church of Canada and the Anglican Communion

Neither the Anglican Communion nor its Canadian province have themselves reflected on ecumenical ministerial formation in a documented way comparable to the WCC or the Catholic Church, although both have a demonstrated commitment to the ecumenical movement, and several theological schools related to the Anglican Church of Canada participate in some form of ecumenical partnership. Notwithstanding the relatively undeveloped

41. Joint Working Group, *Seventh Report*, §21, 15.
42. Joint Working Group, *Seventh Report*, §22.
43. Joint Working Group, *Seventh Report*, §17–18.
44. Joint Working Group, *Seventh Report*, §25.

thinking on ecumenical ministerial formation among Anglicans, I will nevertheless highlight two instances where the issue has been taken up, since the Anglican Church of Canada is the context of my overall research.

One recent official Canadian document that does point to ecumenical formation as an essential aspect of one's ministerial formation is the 2013 *Competencies for Ordination to the Priesthood of the Anglican Church of Canada*. In a reflection of the jurisdictional tension characteristic of the relationship between the General Synod and its constituent dioceses, this national church document goes to some pains to insist that it is not a "set of standards," a "curriculum for theological education," an "ordered checklist," or a "list of all skills that might be needed in all circumstances."[45]

Even so, it was developed at the specific request of the church's bishops, and serves as the only formal set of national guidelines "for those whom the church has called to exercise the ministry of priest in the Anglican Church of Canada."[46] As such, it is significant that among the dozens of competencies sought in a priest, two are that he or she demonstrates "the capacity for effective collaborative leadership and an ability to work in teams in a range of settings, including ecumenical," and also "an awareness of the church's role and opportunities in public life, and a capacity to collaborate in a well-informed way with ecumenical partners, other faith communities and secular agencies."[47]

The Canadian competencies document in part takes its lead and inspiration from the earlier work of the Theological Education in the Anglican Communion (TEAC) working group. While TEAC's mandate includes reflecting on the theological education of the laity as well of future clergy, its most significant contributions have been around developing guidelines for the formation of priests. It does so through what have been dubbed "ministry grids."[48] Developed during the mid 2000s, TEAC's ministry grid

---

45. General Synod, *Competencies*, 6.

46. Strictly speaking this is not entirely true. The preface to the ordinal of the 1962 Canadian *Book of Common Prayer* also stipulates certain prerequisites for candidates to the priesthood. These include that the individual must be "a man of virtuous conversation, and without crime," of sufficient age ("full four-and-twenty years old"), and "learned in holy Scripture, and sufficiently instructed in the Latin tongue . . . ." However, although the Prayer Book canonically remains the official liturgy of the Anglican Church of Canada, its ordination rites are rarely used and its rubrical prescriptions for ordinands—at least those pertaining to gender and Latin proficiency—do not reflect current practice.

47. General Synod, *Competencies*, 19.

48. Anglican Communion, "Ministry Grids."

for priests is comprehensive, naming dozens of general and specific expectations of competencies around vocation and discernment, the nature of ministry, spirituality and faith, character and integrity, relationships, leadership and collaboration, contextual awareness, biblical and theological acumen, and practical abilities. Among these expectations, four have an explicit ecumenical dimension. Among them is the expectation that "ordinands have experienced ecumenical theological education and provision for Anglican teaching and discipline, *vis-à-vis* theology, worship, relation of church and society, and interfaith studies/relations."[49]

Having outlined some of the background of the sources from which I will draw, the discussion can now turn to an exploration of some of the common and fundamental principles of ecumenical ministerial formation to which they give expression. Attention will also be paid to the contributions of individual scholars who have also reflected on this question.

Why Ministerial Ecumenical Formation?

Ecumenical formation is for the whole people of God. Its objective is "that all Christians be animated by the ecumenical spirit, whatever their particular task or mission in the world."[50] The general faith formation of the laity, especially in congregational settings, is normally the responsibility of the community's ordained leader, who has typically received an especially intensive theological and pastoral education. Stephen Bevans articulates a similar understanding of this from a missiological perspective:

> The role of the trained theologian (the minister, the theology teacher) is that of articulating more clearly what the people are expressing more generally or vaguely, deepening their ideas by providing them with the wealth of the Christian tradition, and challenging them to broaden their horizons by presenting them with the whole of Christian theological expression.[51]

Though Bevans is talking here about the process of theological contextualization, the role of the "trained theologian" (i.e., congregational minister) in ecumenical formation is similar. If the laity under a pastor's care are to

---

49. Anglican Communion, "Priests and Transitional Deacons Target Group."
50. PCPUC, *Directory*, §58.
51. Bevans, *Models of Contextual Theology*, 18.

be formed ecumenically, it follows that the pastors themselves receive adequate ecumenical formation:

> If the results of ecumenical dialogue are to be received by the churches, leaders present and future will play a key role in the process. Not only must they be able to inspire interest and assist their people in the understanding of agreed statements, they must also know in their own experience the value of such theology and its applicability to the real pastoral challenges before them.[52]

So key is the role of parish clergy in the ecumenical formation of the faithful they serve, it has been described as nothing less than "the most influential point in ecumenical sensitization."[53] If the ecumenical agreed statements brokered by our churches nationally and internationally fail to find purchase in the churches's most local expressions, then they risk becoming little more than esoteric theological exercises for a relatively small number of ecumenical specialists. Ecumenically educated, conscious, and engaged clergy are an essential variable in cultivating ecumenically educated, conscious, and engaged laity, who will in their local communities of faith be the ones who make the church's unity most tangibly visible.

Curriculum

But what ought ecumenical ministerial formation within the context of a seminary or theological college look like? In its ideal form it is holistic and multidimensional: "such activities as find their locus in the classroom, the seminar room, the library, the common room conversations," but also "all sorts of ecumenical contacts which proceed from outside the normal schedule of the school."[54] Later we will explore extracurricular aspects of ecumenical ministerial formation. Now we attend to the more academic aspects of a cleric's ecumenical learning. For even if ecumenical ministerial formation is more than "simply a matter of including in the curriculum an introductory course on ecumenism,"[55] just such a course remains an essential aspect of the process of one's ecumenical education.

---

52. Flynn, "Ecumenical Dialogue," 5.
53. Joint Working Group, "Fifth Report," 215.
54. Minear, "Import of Ecumenical Developments," 313.
55. Ortega, "Contextuality and Community," 30.

Among those who consider ecumenical ministerial formation important, there is general agreement that a theological student's curriculum ought to contain two explicitly ecumenical aspects: (1) a specific course in ecumenism, and (2) an ecumenical dimension to the teaching of all other theological disciplines. The Catholic Church offers the most detailed example of what such curricula would include.

The purpose of what might be called a "core course" in ecumenism would be "that students clearly understand that the aim of ecumenism is the restoration of full visible unity among all Christians."[56] A course of this kind would include such aspects as biblical foundations for ecumenism, principles of ecumenical engagement (which in the Catholic context would include particular reference to relevant conciliar and papal documents), a history of the ecumenical movement, ecumenical agreed statements (both bilateral and multilateral), ecumenical methods, and spiritual ecumenism.

While the ecumenical *Directory* directs that such a core course should be compulsory, it is difficult to find examples of Roman Catholic seminaries where this is actually the case, or where a course in ecumenism of any kind—mandatory or not—is on offer. Saint Augustine's Seminary, a Roman Catholic major seminary that is a member school of the Toronto School of Theology, periodically offers such a course. However, it is optional and one of its instructors has related anecdotally that her students almost never include seminarians, but rather interested Roman Catholic laypeople. Another Catholic theological educator suggests that this is not uncommon:

> In my experience, if a Catholic seminary or faculty of theology has an introductory course in ecumenism at all, it is usually offered as an elective course where scheduling does not always favor the participation of many. When one attempts to point out the priority of making such a course a requirement for ministerial degree students, one may hear that there are already so many other requirements that this would only add to the already heavy burden that students have in the program. Others may respond that they try to incorporate an ecumenical perspective in all the courses in the calendar and have no need of a special course in ecumenism. Others may reply that budgetary restraints oblige us to limit course offerings. Still others choose to offer special seminars on ecumenical questions, ignoring the need for a basic introduction to the principles of ecumenism.[57]

56. PCPCU, *Ecumenical Dimension*, §25.
57. Clifford, "Wake Up Call," 18.

Ecumenical Theological Education

Wycliffe College, one of the TST's two Anglican colleges, has provided an introductory course in ecumenism.[58] However, it is offered only online and is not compulsory. In contrast, as a part of its relatively new master of divinity program, Ottawa's Saint Paul University offers no fewer than four courses with explicitly ecumenical themes, one of which is mandatory.[59] A more comprehensive view of the ecumenical offerings in the curricula of Canadian Anglican theological schools will be presented in a later chapter.

The intention of a specialized course in ecumenism is not to "create another separate discipline of accumulated knowledge and specialized information," but rather that ecumenism might form "a qualitative dimension of all theological education."[60] Therefore complementing a core course that covers topics like ecumenical history, principles, and method should be the inclusion of an ecumenical aspect to the teaching of all other disciplines of theology covered in the seminary, such as systematic theology, church history, theological ethics or moral theology, biblical studies, ecclesiology, sacramental and liturgical theology, such that "an ecumenical dimension permeates every subject taught"[61] and ecumenism becomes not only a distinct discipline but an "all-pervading orientation" and "a living component in all theological discourse."[62] The Catholic *Directory* puts it this way:

> In every theological discipline an ecumenical approach should bring us to consider the link between the particular subject and the mystery of the unity of the Church. Moreover, the teacher should instil in his students fidelity to the whole authentic Christian Tradition in matters of theology, spirituality and ecclesiastical discipline. When students compare their own patrimony with the riches of the other Christian traditions of East and West, whether in the ancient or modern expression, they will become more deeply conscious of this fullness.[63]

The guidelines even suggest inviting faculty from other denominations to present their respective ecclesial traditions firsthand.[64] Though written from a Catholic perspective, this is an approach that theological educators

---

58. Toronto School of Theology, "Ecumenism."
59. Saint Paul University, "Master of Divinity."
60. Werner, "Ecumenical Formation," 105.
61. PCPCU, *Ecumenical Dimension*, §9
62. Joint Working Group, *Ninth Report*, §§147, 143.
63. PCPCU, *Directory*, §77.
64. PCPCU, *Ecumenical Dimension*, §20(d).

of many other Christian traditions would find salutary and applicable. Indeed, the World Council of Church affirms some of the same principles when it encourages "learning which enables people, while remaining rooted in one tradition of the church, to become open and responsive to the richness and perspectives of other churches, so that they may become more active in seeking unity, openness and collaboration between churches."[65] However, as with the offering of a specialized course in ecumenism, it is questionable to what degree such an ecumenical approach is brought to bear on the teaching of other theological disciplines in most institutions of ministerial formation.

There is another aspect of ecumenical ministerial formation related to curriculum that may at first seem incidental, but can in fact prove highly influential: the one who teaches it: "An ecumenically committed professor or dean has marked the beginning of many lifelong journeys toward unity. During the tenure of one seminary dean, his students remarked that one could not graduate without being thoroughly steeped in ecumenical literature."[66] It is common to hear erstwhile students of the late Margaret O'Gara, many of whom are actively engaged in ecumenical endeavors, bear similar witness to her influence at the TST. I can personally attest to the similarly formative role of John Simons, the retired principal of Montreal Diocesan Theological College.[67]

Extracurricular Dimensions

At least as important as having a specialized course in ecumenism, as well as an ecumenical aspect to all other courses, is ensuring theological students are afforded extracurricular opportunities to engage with other Christian traditions. The Roman Catholic Church's guidelines are insistent on this point: "Genuine ecumenical formation must not remain solely academic; it should also include ecumenical experience."[68] The American Protestant ecumenical scholar Michael Kinnamon puts it more plainly still: "While ecumenism needs to be taught in the classroom, it must also be part of the seminary's general life and self-understanding."[69] Simon Oxley, who coor-

65. Werner, "Ecumenical Formation," 165.
66. Kessler, "Head Change and Heart Work," 5.
67. Myers, "John Simons."
68. PCPCU, *Ecumenical Dimension*, §28.
69. Kinnamon, "Ecumenical Formation," 11.

dinated the WCC's educational and ecumenical formation team between 1996 and 2008, has echoed the need for both what he calls "informal and formal learning," noting that formal courses in ecumenism have value, but typically are not sufficient to cultivate commitment to church unity: "They transmit a certain amount of knowledge of the history, theology and activities of the ecumenical movement but in a dispassionate manner. Students may learn about ecumenism but do not develop ecumenical attitudes."[70]

Indeed, one of the criticisms sometimes leveled at the ecumenical movement as a whole is that it remains in many ways an academic exercise finding relatively little tangible expression. Therefore, ensuring that ecumenical ministerial formation does not begin and end with lectures and seminars enhances the possibility that practical efforts toward visible unity might result when pastors are actually serving local communities.

Once again it is the Roman Catholic Church that has developed the most detailed suggestions on what extracurricular ecumenical opportunities might be offered by a seminary or theological college: organized visits to churches of other traditions, exchanges and joint study days with seminarians of other denominations, guest lecturers from other churches, and occasions for common prayer with other Christians including (but not limited to) the Week of Prayer for Christian Unity.[71] The potential impact of worshipping ecumenically will be explored further in a later chapter, as will the formational significance of ecumenical friendships.

As with the curricular aspects of ecumenical ministerial formation, there is doubt as to how much ecumenical activity of an extracurricular kind is to be found in seminaries or theological colleges—even those which form part of an ecumenical union, consortium, or federation. In 1998 the Canadian Centre for Ecumenism sponsored a survey "to examine the state of ecumenical education in Canada in terms of how ecumenism is being 'taught' in theological faculties and institutes around the country."[72] Among the questions posed to the fifty-four institutions invited to respond was: "To supplement the academic activity of your institute or faculty, do you sponsor extra-academic opportunities (ecumenical prayer, liturgy, social activities, fraternal exchanges, etc.)?" Of the twenty-three responses received, "few institutes did very many of these things, perhaps one or two activities sufficing

---

70. Oxley, *Creative Ecumenical Education*, 113, 121.
71. PCPCU, *Ecumenical Dimension*, §28.
72. Dowd, "Ecumenical Education," 24.

for the most part."[73] Half indicated they did not observe the Week of Prayer for Christian Unity.[74] A subsequent chapter will examine the results of that 1998 survey further, and also delve into the present state of ecumenical formation at Canadian Anglican ministerial training centres.

Practical Outcomes of Ecumenical Ministerial Formation

Among the desired ends of an effective ecumenical ministerial formation are the cultivation in a cleric of a fundamental ecumenical consciousness and orientation that instinctively informs their daily pastoral practice in the local communities they serve. What does such ecumenically informed, on-the-ground pastoral practice look like? What concrete examples of local ecumenical engagement exist that can both serve as benchmarks by which to help measure the degree to which practical ecumenism is finding expression in the church, and also inspire clergy and their congregations to try the same? The following brief literature review will focus on three relatively recent and pertinent publications that help provide answers to these questions. These same documents will help inform an evaluation of the degree to which Canadian Anglican clergy surveyed for this research are themselves ecumenically engaged.

As we have seen in this chapter, the *Directory for the Application of Principles and Norms on Ecumenism* provides concrete examples of "ecumenical cooperation" in all expressions of the Catholic Church—including in priestly formation, but also more widely—while respecting that tradition's teaching and discipline. Other texts make a similar attempt. In *A Handbook of Spiritual Ecumenism*, Cardinal Walter Kasper distills the Catholic Church's teachings on ecumenism since the Second Vatican Council into a slim and accessible volume of "pastoral suggestions" aimed at "finding and fostering the means by which Christian unity can be constructively promoted (. . .)."[75] Another Catholic ecumenist, Paulist Father Thomas Ryan, has been prolific in producing guides for how Christians of all traditions—not only Roman Catholics—might give more visible expression to the church's unity in their own contexts. His latest such effort, *Christian Unity: How You Can Make a Difference*, is much longer and more comprehensive than Kasper's handbook, including spiritual and theological foundations for ecumenism,

---

73. Dowd, "Ecumenical Education," 26.
74. Dowd, "Ecumenical Education," 27.
75. Kasper, *Handbook of Spiritual Ecumenism*, 8–9.

and also "a broad range of grassroots possibilities for the engagement of laity and clergy alike at local levels."[76] These latter two texts—along with a third authored not by an individual but rather a bilateral ecumenical commission—contain recommendations specifically aimed at the parochial expression of the church, and it is on these suggestions that we will soon focus, since the focus of this study is on the ecumenical engagement of clergy whose primary ministry is based in a local congregation.

First, however, one might reasonably ask why a study on the ecumenical formation of Anglican clergy, authored by an Anglican, would rely so heavily on Roman Catholic resources related to the practical application of ecumenical principles. The answer, quite simply, is that no such Anglican resources exist. The closest that the churches of the Anglican Communion come to a document parallel to the Catholic Church's *Directory* is a 2008 text called *The Vision Before Us*. Also known as the Kyoto Report, it is a summary of nearly a decade of work overseen by the worldwide Anglican Communion's Inter-Anglican Standing Commission on Ecumenical Relations. Among other things it catalogues international bilateral and multilateral ecumenical dialogues in which the Anglican Communion was a participant between 2000 and 2008, and highlights the theological themes that were these conversations's focus.

Perhaps this document's most significant contribution to the corpus of Anglican ecumenical literature is its articulation of "Four Principles of Anglican Engagement in Ecumenism," which represents the first detailed and officially endorsed exposition of the theological principles undergirding Anglican ecumenical endeavors. The principles enumerate in turn Anglican ecumenical engagement's (1) goal (the "full visible unity of the church"), (2) task ("to recognize and receive those elements of the one true Church which Anglicans apprehend in their ecumenical partners"), (3) process ("unity by stages"), and (4) content (a common expression of faith and mutually recognized sacraments and ministry as laid out in the Chicago-Lambeth Quadrilateral).[77] At no point, however, does the document attempt—as the Catholic *Directory* does—to further elucidate the nature of this ecumenical content or how it might be expressed in the life and work of the church, especially locally. It does note that "ensuring a greater synergy

---

76. Ryan, *Christian Unity*, xi.
77. Rowland-Jones, *Vision Before Us*, 31–42.

between the international and the local" is one of the "challenges ahead" for Anglican ecumenical engagement.[78]

As its name suggests, the *Code of Practice on Cooperation by the Church of England with Other Churches* is chiefly a regulatory document containing "lists that provide 'recipes' for going about interaction with other churches and that can be used as a checklist for ecumenical activity."[79] As such, the document is heavy on citations of canon law. Among other things it establishes best practices for Church of England parishes entering into formal "ecumenical cooperative schemes" with congregations of other denominations, perhaps one of the most extreme—and visible—manifestations of local ecumenical engagement possible.[80] It also provides guidelines for occasions of joint worship with non-Anglican Christians, the ecumenical use of church buildings, and the recognition of the ministries of clergy from outside the Church of England. However, like *The Vision Before Us*, the English church's document is bereft of any suggestions for practical ecumenical initiatives at the local level, although it does provide the canonical framework to enable them.

The *Handbook for Ecumenism* of the Episcopal Church (the province of the Anglican Communion based in the United States) describes itself as "a tool to help you discern and articulate your roles as bishops and designated ecumenical officers in the unique setting of your diocese in the context of the larger national and worldwide journey toward visible Christian unity."[81] The document summarizes the Episcopal Church's "ecumenical posture and vision," summarizes its historic participation in the ecumenical movement, and outlines its current involvement in bilateral dialogues and councils of churches. Like the Church of England's *Code of Practice*, it also presents the canonical framework for engagement with other denominations. The *Handbook*'s introduction promises "specific suggestions for living ecumenically in your local setting," and while there is a brief section on shared prayer and worship, and a short (and somewhat dated) list of resources on "local ecumenism," these are obscured by what is otherwise a vast collection of historical, structural, and regulatory documents.[82]

---

78. Rowland-Jones, *Vision Before Us*, 239.

79. Church of England, "Code of Practice," §8.

80. In North America these are known as "ecumenical shared ministries," and will be addressed in more detail in a later chapter.

81. Episcopal Church, "Handbook for Ecumenism," 4.

82. Episcopal Church, "Handbook for Ecumenism," 4.

Ecumenical Theological Education

The intention here is not to criticize these three documents. Each in its own way is highly comprehensive in providing historical, theological, and/or canonical foundations and frameworks for Anglican ecumenical engagement, either at a worldwide level or proper to a specific Anglican province's context. However, an individual or community looking for inspiration on exactly how to give concrete expression to the church's full visible unity in their specific local setting will likely be left wanting. Not so with the document we will consider next.

Growing Together in Unity and Mission

A text that does contain both theological foundations for ecumenical engagement and suggestions for the local, practical outworking of those principles—and which also has some level of formal approbation in the Anglican Communion—is *Growing Together in Unity and Mission* (GTUM). Published in 2007, it is the foundational document of the International Anglican-Roman Catholic Commission on Unity and Mission (IARCCUM). Established in 2001 following a formal meeting of Anglican and Roman Catholic bishops a year earlier in Mississauga, Ontario, convened by the Archbishop of Canterbury and the President of the Pontifical Council for Promoting Christian Unity, IARCCUM's mandate is to "promote our relationship by seeking to translate our manifest agreement in faith into common life and mission."[83] In their introduction to the document, the commission's Anglican and Roman Catholic co-chairs described GTUM as not just an ecumenical document for discussion and reflection, but rather nothing less than a "call for action."[84]

GTUM is divided into two sections. The first, labelled "The Achievements of Anglican-Roman Catholic Dialogue," summarizes this "manifest agreement in faith," harvesting the fruits of four decades of official theological dialogue between Anglicans and Roman Catholics on the Trinity, communion ecclesiology, scripture, sacraments, ministry, authority, discipleship, and the Blessed Virgin Mary. The document also candidly identifies "where further theological work is necessary" in each of these areas, and where agreement has remained elusive.[85] What makes GTUM relatively unique in the genre of ecumenical texts is that it consciously makes the turn from

83. IARCCUM, *Growing Together*, Preface.
84. IARCCUM, *Growing Together*, Preface.
85. IARCCUM, *Growing Together*, §9.

cataloguing theological agreement to outlining its concrete implications for the dialogue partners, and it does with a particular sense of imperative:

> Genuine faith is more than assent: it is expressed in action. As Anglicans and Roman Catholics seek to overcome the remaining obstacles to full visible unity, we, the bishops of IARCCUM, recognize that the extent of common faith described in this statement compels us to live and witness together more fully here and now. Agreement in faith must go beyond mere affirmation. Discerning a common faith challenges our churches to recognize that elements of sanctification and truth exist in each other's ecclesial lives, and to develop those channels and practical expressions of cooperation by which a common life and mission may be generated and sustained.[86]

Suggestions for such practical expressions of cooperation—"the kind of joint action in mission that we believe our shared faith now invites us to pursue and which would deepen the communion we share"[87]—form the substance of GTUM's second section, "Towards Unity and Common Mission." This section is in turn divided into four categories, each of which contains a number of suggested practices. Although GTUM's focus is on what Anglicans and Roman Catholics can do together, many of its suggestions can be generalized for a broader ecumenical audience. For the purposes of clarity and comparison, the practical recommendations offered by each of the three documents, including GTUM, will be detailed in a table below.

A Handbook of Spiritual Ecumenism

Walter Kasper's short volume follows a similar pattern to GTUM, with each chapter first offering rationales for ecumenical engagement grounded in scripture, theology, and official Catholic teaching, followed by practical suggestions flowing from those foundations. It is intended for a popular audience—"everyone who has at heart the restoration of unity among Christians"[88]—and as such the suggested practices extend beyond what only Anglicans and Roman Catholics might do together, based on the existing level of agreement in the faith among many divided Christians. Each section of the handbook concludes with, "Together, Christians can . . ."

---

86. IARCCUM, *Growing Together*, §96
87. IARCCUM, *Growing Together*, §99.
88. Kasper, *Handbook of Spiritual Ecumenism*, 9.

Ecumenical Theological Education

followed by a list of possible ecumenical activities, which are compiled in the table below.

Acknowledging the key role of the clergy in ecumenical formation, Kasper, a former president of the Pontifical Council for Promoting of Christian Unity, also includes a brief separate chapter of suggestions of ecumenical engagement specifically for pastoral ministers, noting that the example they set is "the most convincing teaching that the faithful can receive in matters of Christian unity."[89] Among other things it suggests local clergy of different traditions gather regularly for prayer and fraternal exchange, and also "show solidarity when something important happens in the private or pastoral life of ministers of other traditions living in the same local area."[90]

Christian Unity: How You Can Make a Difference

Thomas Ryan's is the final text we will review for its recommendations for practical ecumenical expressions in a congregational setting. The pattern for his *Christian Unity: How You Can Make a Difference* is similar to the previous two documents. His book begins with two chapters laying out the biblical, theological, and magisterial grounds for ecumenism, which are followed by eight further "'action' chapters" that take the reader "from the cerebral to the concrete," relating through personal narratives and interviews "a very down-to-earth picture of the different forms that being an active agent for reconciliation in the Body of Christ can take."[91] For reasons evident from its title, it is the first of these "'action' chapters"—"What *You* Can Do—Parishes/Congregations"—that will be our focus. It includes a thirty-three-point list of suggestions for local ecumenical projects or gestures which he describes as "modestly ambitious," cautioning that overly ambitious initiatives often never materialize, and that humbler endeavors can "demonstrate that ecumenism has to do with some very ordinary experiences in the local parish community."[92] Ryan's suggestions specifically are related to the context of a local congregation, and are also summarized in the table below.

Ryan concludes his list by suggesting that congregations try "cultivating an awareness of each other's gifts," and takes up the theme of ecumenical

89. Kasper, *Handbook of Spiritual Ecumenism*, 87.
90. Kasper, *Handbook of Spiritual Ecumenism*, 88.
91. Ryan, *Christian Unity*, xi.
92. Ryan, *Christian Unity*, 56.

gifts in more detail later in the book. It is an idea most recently developed by Catholic ecumenist Paul Murray in what he has coined "receptive ecumenism," which he describes as reversal of the customary approach of ecumenical dialogue in the style of a famous axiom of former U.S. President John F. Kennedy: "Ask not what your ecumenical others need to learn from you; ask rather what your tradition can learn and needs to learn from your ecumenical others."[93] It is also an approach that could be said to be patterned on Jesus' teaching about taking the plank out of one's own eye before pointing out the speck in the eye of someone else.[94] This method is being applied to the work of at least two bilateral ecumenical dialogues at the national and international level, but Murray's expectation is that receptive ecumenism would also find purchase locally, in existing interchurch activities such as ministerial fraternities, Lenten groups, and ecumenical scripture-sharing groups. Receptive ecumenism, he stresses, is not about simply one Christian tradition learning about another, but rather about "learning what one tradition, in the light of its own specific difficulties and challenges, might learn and receive in real terms *from* another tradition."[95] So, for example, a local group of aging Anglicans might ask what they have to learn from a local and thriving evangelical church about youth ministry, and those same evangelical Christians might ask what gifts they might receive from Anglicanism's sacramental and liturgical tradition.

Looking broadly at the practical suggestions offered by IARCCUM, Kasper, and Ryan, one notes the width of scope, even when only considering those recommendations more specifically aimed at congregations. They cover practically every sphere of parochial life and work—everything from catechesis to worship, pastoral care to public witness, social justice to social events. This breadth reflects one of the fundamental precepts of the modern ecumenical movement, the Lund Principle, which exhorts the churches to "act together in all matters except those in which deep differences of conviction compel them to act separately."[96] It is sometimes ruefully remarked that the churches usually operate with a reversed version of the Lund Principal, acting together only perfunctorily or when absolutely necessary. However, Ryan points out that if the churches earnestly applied

---

93. Murray, "ARCIC III," 209.
94. See Matt 7:3–5. I owe this biblical insight to Scott Sharman.
95. Murray, "In Search of a Way." Emphasis in original.
96. West, "Lund Principle," 714–15.

the Lund Principle in their daily life and work, "there would not be that many things that we would have to do separately."[97]

The three documents's practical recommendations are presented in the table below. I have attempted to organize them in the four broad categories of activities used by GTUM: "visible expressions of our shared faith," "joint study of our faith," "cooperation in ministry," and "shared witness in the world." Although some of the suggestions do not necessarily fall neatly into a single category, presenting the recommendations side by side does help illustrate the degree to which the documents agree on the kind of local ecumenical engagement that is both desirable and possible.

---

97. Ryan, *Christian Unity*, 46.

Table 1: Comparison of suggestions for practical ecumenical engagement included in *Growing Together in Unity and Mission*, *A Handbook of Spiritual Ecumenism*, and *Christian Unity: How You Can Make a Difference*

	Growing Together in Unity and Mission	A Handbook of Spiritual Ecumenism	Christian Unity: How You Can Make a Difference
"Visible expressions of our shared faith"	• Joint catechetical programs and common resources for Sunday school, baptismal and confirmation preparation;	• Develop common initiatives among local communities in catechesis and continuing formation;	• Social gatherings to which other Christians may be invited;
	• Local parishes making a regular, common profession of faith, such as renewing baptismal promises at Pentecost;	• Hold an ecumenical affirmation or commemoration of baptism;	• Extending invitations to neighboring churches to attend baptisms in a communal setting as representatives of the wider Body of Christ;
	• A common local baptismal certificate;	• Organize specific days dedicated to the Bible, such as "Bible Sunday" for parishes;	• Church socials, suppers, fundraisers, and picnics as an expression of Christian sharing;
	• Encouraging witnesses from the other church at baptisms and confirmations;	• Commemorate ecumenically local saints who were instrumental in the original spreading of the gospel in a particular region;	• Exchanging news between local churches through parish bulletins;

	Growing Together in Unity and Mission	A Handbook of Spiritual Ecumenism	Christian Unity: How You Can Make a Difference
"Visible expressions of our shared faith"	• Attendance at each other's eucharists (while "respecting the different disciplines of our churches"); • More frequent joint non-eucharistic worship, such as pilgrimages, processions of witness (such as Good Friday), and shared public liturgies on significant occasions; • Praying for each other's local bishops, and including the Pope and Archbishop of Canterbury in the prayers of the people at public eucharistic celebrations.	• Insert particular intercessions for Christian unity in the liturgical prayers of the church; • Pray together during the Week of Prayer for Christian Unity, on the occasion of ecumenical gatherings, during some important periods of the liturgical year (e.g. Advent, Christmas, Lent, and Easter), in remembrance of the dead or those who died for their country, in times of public disaster or mourning, on significant days in the life of other churches (like the Sunday of Orthodoxy or Reformation Sunday), or on particular days in public or social life (e.g. New Year's Day, the beginning or end of a school year, harvest thanksgiving); • Exchange delegates or messages between local communities on particular occasions, such as ordinations and funerals.	• Placing greetings for feasts like Christmas and Easter jointly with other churches in a local newspaper; • Placing holy day greetings to other local religious communities (e.g. Jewish and Muslim) jointly with other churches in a local newspaper; • Organizing an ecumenical concert, combining local churches's choirs.

Formation for Transformation

	Growing Together in Unity and Mission	A Handbook of Spiritual Ecumenism	Christian Unity: How You Can Make a Difference
"Joint study of our faith"	• Joint study of the scriptures, "particularly by those in training for ministry";	• Read and meditate upon particular books of the Bible in small groups;	• Planning a tour of local churches, with commentary offered on each one's devotional particularities, worship space, furnishings, style, etc.
	• Joint Bible study groups based on our similar Sunday lectionaries;	• Conduct Bible courses organized by and conducted together with neighboring parish communities.	• Exchange speakers among local congregations;
	• Lectures/workshops on different methodological approaches to the scriptures;		• Occasionally attend worship in other local congregations;
	• Joint workshops for preachers and shared study of each other's liturgical traditions;		• Offering a joint vacation church/ Bible school;
	• Joint studies of the work of the Anglican-Roman Catholic International Commission;		• Planning leadership training in evangelism, stewardship, or advocacy with other congregations;
	• Establishing regional or local Anglican-Roman Catholic dialogues where they do not already exist;		• Cultivating an awareness of each other's gifts.

Ecumenical Theological Education

	Growing Together in Unity and Mission	A Handbook of Spiritual Ecumenism	Christian Unity: How You Can Make a Difference
"Joint study of our faith"	• Sharing professional staff, libraries, and formation and study programs for clergy and laity.		
"Cooperation in ministry"	• Establishing a regional or local Anglican-Roman Catholic bishops's dialogue where they do not already exist;	• Develop marriage preparation programs specifically aimed at inter-church couples "to better understand each partner's religious convictions and deepen their shared Christian inheritance";	• Organizing exchanges between comparable lay congregational organizations;
	• Inviting observers to attend each other's synodical and collegial gatherings and conferences;	• Work together in chaplaincy and pastoral care in locations such as hospitals, prisons, or refugee camps;	• Establishing an ecumenical "welcome and visitation committee" that would collectively welcome and offer support to newcomers to the neighborhood;
	• Issuing joint pastoral statements on urgent matters of common concern at the regional and national levels;	• Communicate information between local communities about major events, particular celebrations, and specific programs;	• Sharing educational facilities, tools, and resources;

	Growing Together in Unity and Mission	A Handbook of Spiritual Ecumenism	Christian Unity: How You Can Make a Difference
"Cooperation in ministry"	• Having neighboring Anglican bishops accompany their Roman Catholic counterparts on their *ad limina* visits to Rome; • Establishing protocols for the movement of clergy from one communion to the other; • Joint formation for ministry, particularly for newly ordained bishops; • Cooperation in the theological education of priests, especially in the fields of biblical studies, church history, and pastoral formation; • Joint diaconal training; • Ongoing clergy formation, including joint clergy retreats;	• Develop common initiatives among local communities in the pastoral care of particular people (e.g. those in hospital, university students), evangelization, and outreach to the marginalized.	• Gathering together local congregational leaders for a retreat or daylong meeting to discuss joint activities in worship, education, and/or service; • Organizing youth ministries together, particularly when individual congregations have small numbers of youth; • Offering an ecumenical support group for interchurch families.

	Growing Together in Unity and Mission	A Handbook of Spiritual Ecumenism	Christian Unity: How You Can Make a Difference
"Cooperation in ministry"	• Attending each other's ordinations; • Strengthening relations between Anglican and Roman Catholic religious communities, particularly those which share a common founder (e.g. Benedictines and Franciscans); • Developing programs of joint pastoral care for interchurch families, including marriage preparation; • Joint training for lay ministries, such as catechists, lectors, readers, teachers, and evangelists; • Sharing the talents and resources of lay ministers between local Anglican and Roman Catholic parishes, including music ministries.		

	Growing Together in Unity and Mission	A Handbook of Spiritual Ecumenism	Christian Unity: How You Can Make a Difference
"Shared witness in the world"	• Urging our two communions to work together globally with others to promote social justice, eradicate poverty, and care for the environment; • Encouraging churches locally in their social witness to "do all things together excepting only those things that deep differences compel us to do separately"; • Express together a willingness to repent of our actions and work toward reconciliation when we as churches have been guilty of contribution to tensions and strife of a political, socio-economic, or religious nature; • Joint participation in evangelism, including the shared training of lay people for evangelism;	• Joint mission to those who have never heard the gospel of Jesus Christ and in evangelization of those whose faith is challenged by contemporary secular society; • Use every possible means to relieve those suffering from famine and natural disasters, illiteracy and poverty, lack of housing and the unequal distribution of wealth; • Engaging together in interreligious dialogue, especially given its increasing importance in many parts of the world.	• Sponsoring joint studies on issues confronting the local community, such as hunger, economic justice, racism, and human rights; • Initiating service projects among area churches to collectively respond to needs such as housing, unemployment, transportation for the elderly and disabled, and care for refugees; • Forming ecumenical community task forces on problems such as drug use, runaways, nursing homes, or child/spouse abuse; • Expressing Christian concern by taking up a collection on the same day in all churches in the neighborhood for a cause that has commanded the attention of the local community.

	Growing Together in Unity and Mission	A Handbook of Spiritual Ecumenism	Christian Unity: How You Can Make a Difference
"Shared witness in the world"	• Developing joint Anglican–Roman Catholic church schools, shared teacher training programs, and contemporary religious education curricula; • Working more closely together in relations with adherents of other religions.		

The table helpfully demonstrates how these three distinct works share common themes about what Christians of different traditions can and ought to do together. A particular consensus appears with respect to activities connected to baptism, such as joint baptismal preparation, joint commemorations of baptism, joint renewals of baptismal promises, and the development of common baptismal certificates. This is perhaps unsurprising given the Second Vatican Council's emphasis on baptism as the sacramental bond that binds all Christian together despite ecclesial divisions.[98] The three texts also strongly emphasize ecumenical common prayer and joint study of the Bible. Shared outreach to marginalized members of society is also a recurring theme. Essentially the three sets of suggested practices give detailed expression to the Lund Principle—churches doing all things together but those things which deep differences oblige them to do apart—which both GTUM and Ryan explicitly name.

These practical suggestions will be revisited in a later chapter, when we attempt to evaluate the extent to which the ecumenical formation of the clergy surveyed in this study has resulted in actual ecumenical engagement in their current ministries.

'Transformational' Ecumenical Formation

This chapter has traced the origins of ecumenical theological education back to the seminal World Missionary Conference of 1910 and reviewed its subsequent development within the thinking of the World Council of Churches, the Roman Catholic Church, and (to a lesser extent) the Anglican Communion. Organizational models of ecumenical theological education, particularly in Canada, were also explored. There has also been a preliminary discussion about the degree to which the ideals of ecumenical ministerial formation articulated by its advocates have in fact found expression in the curricula and other aspects of life at seminaries and theological colleges affiliated with the Anglican Church of Canada. The practical expressions of ecumenism, which are in part the desired outcome of an effective ecumenical ministerial formation, were also explored by reviewing three relatively recent documents that promote concrete forms of ecumenical engagement at the local level of the church.

Advocates and practitioners of ecumenical ministerial formation are persuaded that a particular constellation of curricular and extracurricular

---

98 *Unitatis Redintegratio*, §3.

variables in a student's theological education can result in a pastor who is not only ecumenically aware, but utterly transformed and converted to exercising a ministry giving expression in every possible way to revealing the church's visible unity. These elements include a core course in ecumenism, an ecumenical dimension to the teaching of all other theological disciplines, faculty and fellow students from other Christian traditions, ecumenical common prayer, and even the development of ecumenical friendships. Some of the means by which the conditions for what has been described by some as a transformational ministerial formation can be created will be explored in the next chapter, as will a pedagogical theory from the realm of adult education that provides some relevant insights.

3

Transformative Learning

A CONSISTENT THEME AMONG those who have deeply engaged with the question of ministerial ecumenical formation, as seen in the literature already reviewed, is the conviction that this process must not simply consist of individuals being taught about ecumenism. Rather, one's ecumenical learning must be holistic and experiential in its approach. The World Council of Churches (WCC) has over the decades dedicated significant resources to study and reflection on ecumenical formation, and is representative of the many voices insistent on a fulsome educational approach: "[E]cumenical learning cannot be limited to mere communication of facts, history, background, structures and functions of the ecumenical movement. Rather, it is the comprehensive task of equipping Christians to live as a liberating and reconciling community in a divided world."[1]

It is no coincidence that in this statement one might detect echoes of the thinking of the noted Brazilian educator and activist Paolo Freire. He worked with the WCC's Office of Education throughout the 1970s and significantly influenced the ecumenical movement's approach to ecumenical learning. This included a definitive turning away from more customary teaching models: "In contrast to the 'banking' model, where the student is a passive receptacle of knowledge, Freire's method prioritized the concrete and immediate experience of the student and encouraged them to reflect critically on their experience, challenge the status quo and take control of their own destiny."[2]

---

1. World Council of Churches, *Nairobi to Vancouver*, 183.
2. Graham et al., *Theological Reflection*, 183.

Freire's educational method, known as *conscientização* or "critical consciousness," had as its goal "reversing the cycles of fatality and passivity and moving towards empowerment."³ As Freire himself put it in his seminal work on this theory, *Pedagogy of the Oppressed*, the banking model of education effectively guarantees a perpetuation of the societal status quo:

> The more students work at storing the deposits entrusted to them, the less they develop the critical consciousness which would result from their intervention in the world as transformers of that world. The more completely they accept the passive role imposed on them, the more they tend simply to adapt to the world as it is and to the fragmented view of reality deposited in them.⁴

Freire's concept quickly found purchase with liberation theologians who were his Latin American contemporaries, and who were seeking tools with which to challenge oppressive regimes in that region of the world. However, ecumenists also resonated with his holistic and experiential approach to education. What Freire would have described as education for liberation, some ecumenists have taken to describe as education for transformation—both standing in contrast to a model of education by which teachers simply attempt to download knowledge to their students: "Unlike education as transmission, where the learners acquire a greater quantity of information, education as transformation results in a qualitative change in the learners and their contexts."⁵

It is notable how often advocates of this model of ecumenical formation use the language or idea of the personal transformation of the learner. The late Canadian ecumenist, Margaret O'Gara, is representative of this when she observed thirty years ago, "My eighteen years of teaching divinity students has convinced me of the power that teaching can have when it is carried out in the context of a total personal formation. Done in the right way, formation plus information yield something new: transformation."⁶

How is such a transformation achieved, how is it defined, and what would such a holistic approach to ecumenical ministerial formation in particular look like? Before exploring these questions within the context of the theological education of those preparing for ordination, we will briefly

---

3. Graham et al., *Theological Reflection*, 183.
4. Freire, *Pedagogy of the Oppressed*, 73.
5. Oxley, *Creative Ecumenical Education*, 17.
6. O'Gara, "Formation for Transformation," 23.

look at the leading pedagogical theory that has developed around this idea of education as a means of transformation.

Transformative Learning Theory

The theory of transformative learning[7] in the field of adult education was first developed in the 1990s by American sociologist Jack Mezirow (himself influenced by Friere), who has defined it as "the process by which we transform our taken-for-granted frames of reference (meaning perspectives, habits of mind, mind-sets) to make them more inclusive, discriminating, open, emotionally capable of change, and reflective so that they may generate beliefs and opinions that will prove more true or justified to guide action."[8] At the conclusion of this process, an individual will have experienced a *perspective transformation*, that is, "a permanent change in the foundation of one's beliefs, values, commitments, and conduct."[9]

These frames of reference are "the structures of assumptions through which we understand our experiences."[10] Chiefly the result of cultural assimilation and the influence of primary caregivers, and therefore deep seated, frames of reference have of two dimensions. *Habits of mind* are a set of codes (cultural, social, educational, economic, political, or psychological) that influence an individual's way of thinking, feeling, and acting. A *point of view*, which develops out of one's habits of mind, is "the constellation of belief, value judgement, attitude, and feeling that shapes a particular interpretation."[11]

Ethnocentrism is an example Mezirow uses to illustrate the relationship between habits of mind and a point of view. A predisposition to regard as inferior others who are not a part of one's own in-group is a habit of mind. The point of view that might emerge from this habit of mind "is the complex of feelings, beliefs, judgements, and attitudes we have regarding specific individuals or groups (for example, homosexuals, welfare recipients, people of color, or women)."[12]

---

7. This theory is also sometimes referred to as "transformational learning." In relevant literature the two terms seem to be used interchangeably. "Transformative" is used here, since that is the term used by Mezirow.

8. Mezirow, "Learning to Think," 7–8.

9. Young, "Transformational Learning," 322.

10. Mezirow, "Transformative Learning," 5.

11. Mezirow, "Transformative Learning," 5–6.

12. Mezirow, "Transformative Learning," 6.

Transformative Learning

Mezirow enumerates ten steps or phases in the process leading to a perspective transformation, a permanent change in an individual's frames of reference. The process is put into motion by a disorienting dilemma, followed by self-examination, critical assessment of assumptions, recognition of others's similar transformations, an exploration of options, a plan of action, the acquisition of knowledge and skills, provisional efforts, building of confidence, and reintegration into one's life of the newly acquired perspective.[13]

The process of transformation cannot begin without an individual experiencing a disorienting event or dilemma. This can be an intensely emotional ordeal, since it typically involves calling into question one's cherished beliefs and becoming aware of the deep-seated assumptions undergirding those beliefs.[14] When these foundations and understandings of reality are challenged by an experience that contradicts them, "individuals cannot avoid wondering, questioning, and doubting. The discomfort of inner conflict compels them on a personal journey to make sense of their newly changed world."[15]

These disorienting dilemmas can take many forms from the immediate and dramatic (what Mezirow calls "epochal" transformation[16]) to the gradual and seemingly mundane (or "incremental" transformation, again using Mezirow's terminology[17]). James Loder, for example, describes the transforming effect his near-death experience in a car accident had on his decision to pursue ordination.[18] Less dramatic and more gradual is an example, cited by Edward Taylor, of a woman who previously harboured a negative attitude toward feminists, but then eventually came to self-identify as a feminist herself after a combination of events that included giving birth, developing a close relationship with a "highly intellectual and nurturing feminist," and participating in a women's studies class.[19]

---

13. Mezirow, "Learning to Think," 22. Other accounts of transformational learning articulate similar phases in the process, but use different terminology. For example, Mezirow's "disorienting dilemma" is referred to in other studies as a "trigger event" (Brookfield, *Developing Critical Thinkers*), an "activating event" (Cranton, "Teaching for Transformation"), a "conflict" (Loder), or "cognitive dissonance" (Tite), yet all refer to an identifiable disruptive experience setting the transformative process into action.

14. Mezirow, "Learning to Think," 7, 24.

15. Young, "Transformational Learning," 323–24.

16. Mezirow, "Learning to Think," 21.

17. Mezirow, "Learning to Think," 21.

18. James Loder, *Transforming Moment*, 9–13.

19. Taylor, "Analyzing Research," 299.

Returning to the example of ethnocentrism, Mezirow explains two ways by which such a frame of reference might be transformed. The first is what he calls an "accretion of transformations in points of view":

> We can have an experience in another culture [the disorienting dilemma] that results in our critically reflecting on our misconceptions of this particular group. The result may be a change in point of view toward the group involved. As a result, we may become more tolerant or more accepting of members of that group. If this happens over and over again with a number of different groups, it can lead to a transformation by accretion in our governing habit of mind.[20]

The other, less common and more difficult means of effecting a perspective transformation is by "becoming aware and critically reflective of our generalized bias in the way we view groups other than our own."[21] Either way, the result is a permanent change in the way the individual believes and behaves with respect to the frame of reference being challenged, in this case an inclination to take a lesser view of those who do not belong to one's in-group.

Bossey: Transformative Learning in an Ecumenical Setting

It is not difficult to see how the insights of transformative learning theory might be applied to ecumenical ministerial formation. In naming some of the sets of codes that program an individual's habits of mind, Mezirow mentions cultural, social, educational, economic, political, and psychological.[22] For the purposes of this discussion we could easily add *ecclesial* to that list of codes. Mezirow's example of ethnocentrism can be similarly extended. He defines ethnocentrism as "the predisposition to regard others outside one's own group as inferior," and lists some of these possible "others": homosexuals, welfare recipients, people of color, and women.[23] That list too could be extended from an ecclesial standpoint to include, for example, Roman Catholics, Anglicans, Lutherans, Oriental Orthodox, and Evangelicals—each a group within the Christian church that is considered inferior or somehow deficient (theologically, ecclesiologically, or sacramentally, for example) by

---

20. Mezirow, "Transformative Learning," 7.
21. Mezirow, "Transformative Learning," 7.
22. Mezirow, "Transformative Learning," 6.
23. Mezirow, "Transformative Learning," 6.

members of other groups.[24] How then could the frame of reference of, for example, a Roman Catholic who believes that Anglicans are heretics and excluded from salvation be changed in such a way as they might instead understand Anglicans as (to borrow the language of the Second Vatican Council) "separated brethren" bound together by a common baptism, and occupying "a special place" among the churches of the Reformation?[25]

One place that might offer a clue is the Ecumenical Institute at Bossey, Switzerland. Since 1946 this educational institution of the World Council of Churches has drawn together women and men from every region of the world and most every Christian tradition for a fully residential program of study. Students not only participate in formal academic courses in ecumenics, but they also share accommodations, meals, social time, field trips, Bible study, and worship. These "intentionally interdependent patterns of activity" are deliberately designed to "develop an ecumenical perspective and commitment among the participants."[26] The institute's relatively secluded location, in the Swiss countryside outside Geneva, helps engender an environment "where almost none of the participants is genuinely at home."[27] The Ecumenical Institute's longtime director, himself a former Bossey student, acknowledges the intense nature of this particular form of ecumenical learning, and is fond of describing the dislocating experience as a form of "shock therapy" through which students are exposed not only to new and different ecclesial traditions, but also different ethnicities, cultures, and social mores. This exposure frequently and unsurprisingly results in conflict—both internal and external—as he relates in this account of his own initial experiences as an Eastern Orthodox student at the Ecumenical Institute:

> I still remember the first morning in the Bossey chapel together with colleagues from all over the world and from most of the Christian confessions. Everything I experienced was so different, challenging and even disturbing. During that morning prayer, we

---

24. There are also groups *within* each of these ecclesial families that would consider others who share a common name and heritage as inferior and deficient. For example, Missouri Synod Lutherans consider mainline Lutheran churches theologically lacking; Anglicans belonging to the Fellowship of Confessing Anglicans question the orthodoxy of several provinces of the Anglican Communion; and certain expressions of Catholicism doubt the validity of the teaching and authority of the Catholic Church following the Second Vatican Council.

25. *Unitatis Redintegratio*, §1, §13.

26. Gilligan, "Does What Is Taught," 39–40.

27. Gilligan, "Does What Is Taught," 39–40.

were given a piece of paper and asked to write down an offence done to somebody, a burden or a sin that we have committed. And we were invited to put the papers together on the stony floor in the middle of the chapel. The leader of the worship said a prayer of absolution above the pile of papers and then lit them. While the papers with our sins were burning, we were asked to come around in a circle around the fire, to clap hands and dance singing the Orthodox responsive hymn "Kyrie eleison." At first, I did not know what to do and I remember having very quick reflection on how I should behave: "If I refuse to join the others in their symbolic action," I said to myself, "they will think that I am anti-ecumenical and I would be badly perceived and judged; if I do what they are doing and dance in a church around a fire, God will be upset with me and my salvation will be at stake." So, I joined the circle, I moved slowly left and right with the others and pretended to clap my hands. But I felt very bad and guilty. Similar shocking experiences came almost every day. I was so disturbed and discouraged that I thought of leaving Bossey and going home to save my faith from compromise and not to lose my salvation. But I continued to pray, asking God for a sign if what I was doing was wrong and waited with patience. And this is how my new birth has started.[28]

Even in this relatively short account one can detect points of contact with Mezirow's transformative learning theory. That morning's ritual in the Bossey chapel was the disorienting dilemma that triggered an ongoing process of re-evaluation that permanently changed this individual's frames of reference with respect to non-Orthodox Christians, calling it nothing less than being born again. As the institute's director, he sought to accompany others through their own jarring journeys of transformation at Bossey: "As my formation came out of a kind of 'shock therapy,' I tried to help and accompany the many other students today who are having the same challenging experience when they first arrive here. And though the challenges and hardships are many every day, the satisfaction of seeing how lives are being transformed is rewarding and encouraging."[29]

Such experiences are not uncommon among Bossey graduates. In 2013 the Ecumenical Institute published a collection of testimonies submitted by former students. It is notable how often the language of transformation (or similar terminology) is used in these accounts:

---

28. Sauca, *Place to Remember*, 43.
29. Sauca, *Place to Remember*, 3.

Transformative Learning

- "My academic and religious journey at Bossey has been a transforming factor in this process: It has made me open up and reach out to people and leaders of other faiths, while still holding onto my Christian beliefs and core values."[30]
- "Altogether the time I spent in Bossey was a life-transforming experience."[31]
- "As I left Bossey, I was transformed."[32]
- "Bossey [is] a place that transforms."[33]
- "Bossey is a place that indeed transforms, strengthens and enhances identities."[34]
- "My two stints at Bossey indeed have strengthened, transformed and enhanced our work to build a just, compassionate and responsible society in the Philippines."[35]
- "I cannot exaggerate the life-changing consequences of my time at Bossey."[36]
- "The Bossey experience is a life-changing experience."[37]
- "I left Bossey changed."[38]
- "[M]y life was changed forever in terms of my outlook on human interaction, education and ecumenism."[39]
- "I have never been the same since Bossey days."[40]
- "Bossey has made me 'born again' as regards my attitudes towards Christians of other church affiliations."[41]

---

30. Acquah, *Place to Remember*, 5.
31. Damian, *Place to Remember*, 18.
32. Gatu, *Place to Remember*, 22.
33. Kalu in *Place to Remember*, 29.
34. Nagypál, *Place to Remember*, 36.
35. Senturias, *Place to Remember*, 45.
36. Bosch, *Place to Remember*, 14.
37. Chavez Quispe, *Place to Remember*, 40.
38. Spiller, *Place to Remember*, 48.
39. Bwalya, *Place to Remember*, 16.
40. Durham, *Place to Remember*, 20.
41. Tindyebwa Francis, *Place to Remember*, 21.

- "[Bossey] would change my entire life, my understanding of church and my direction in ministry."[42]

These strikingly similar testimonies come from individuals hailing from a diversity of places (Canada, Bolivia, Ghana, Hungary, Kenya, New Zealand, Nigeria, the Philippines, Romania, Tanzania, the United Kingdom, the United States, and Zambia) representing a variety of Christian traditions (Anglican, Eastern Orthodox, Lutheran, Methodist, Presbyterian, Reformed, Roman Catholic, and United). For some, the permanent, life-changing consequences of their transformative Bossey experience have included a reorientation of academic studies, a change in ministry or career path, and at least two interchurch marriages between individuals who met while students at the Ecumenical Institute.

Similar observations emerged from a survey of Bossey graduates from the United States, conducted by a group of American ecumenical scholars in 1996, on the occasion of the institute's fiftieth anniversary: "The words 'life-changing,' even 'magical,' appeared in our surveys more frequently that might be expected from a group of highly educated respondents with graduate degrees."[43] In the same collection of research, other former Bossey students variously described the process of moving from disorienting dilemma to having their frame of reference transformed as "cognitive dissonance," "controlled alienation," and "growth through sorrow."[44]

One American Bossey alumna described her learning experience at the institute as "a process catalyzed by provocation."[45] For her, the provocative presenting issue (i.e. disorienting dilemma) was women's ordination, which for her, as an ordained woman, was one of her most significant religious values and deeply held concerns. However, she discovered that among some of her Bossey classmates "this conviction was a strange curiosity; it was an irrelevant issue for others struggling against women's illiteracy and for their basic human rights; for still others it was a heretical position."[46] Having what she described as her "unexamined assumptions" on women's ordination challenged by her fellow students prompted her to

---

42. Welsh, *Place to Remember*, 53.
43. Lindner and Delloff, "U.S. Bossey Assessment Project," 6.
44. Delloff, "Embracing Estrangement," 17.
45. Wood, "Learning a Religious Tradition," 33.
46. Wood, "Learning a Religious Tradition," 34.

Transformative Learning

both re-examine her own theological premises and appreciate how those of other traditions might hold a different view:

> I would have described [my denomination's] tradition and my own beliefs as liberal, non-parochial, open to embracing within the faith community a diversity of perspectives and beliefs. Yet when I found myself as obstinate about my tradition's perspectives about emerging ideas of women in the church as others were about their tradition's adherence to traditional roles, I became aware of how parochial, in fact, we can all be about matters as important as our religious convictions.[47]

While her own views on women's ordination did not change, her perspective of other Christians not sharing her opinion did—a transformation she suggests would not have occurred without the provocation of sustained encounters and relationship with those others: "I needed to be provoked to see myself from the perspective of the other. Whatever the constitutive elements of one's total identity, we often take them for granted unless provoked to define them explicitly."[48] Her account of the experience—and even some of the terminology she uses to describe it—in many ways mirrors Mezirow's stages leading to a perspective transformation.

The publication of the 2013 Bossey testimonials was not in any way an attempt to test transformative learning theory, and those solicited for contributions were not specifically asked to reflect on their experience at the institute in such terms. Nevertheless, several did describe some of the elements that contributed to what Mezirow might describe as a permanent change in their frame of reference with respect to Christians of other traditions:

- "Sharing our different cultural values and experiences through food, dancing and art made me feel that we are members of each other's society, a thing that I consider crucial in building good relationships between Christians of different confessions."[49]

- "*Vivre à Bossey, ce n'est pas seulement étudier, mais aussi participer à toutes sortes d'activités culturelles, découvrir l'église de l'autre, son culte et sa théologie, s'impliquer aussi dans la vie de la maison. Peu à*

---

47. Wood, "Learning a Religious Tradition," 35.
48. Wood, "Learning a Religious Tradition," 33.
49. Tindyebwa Francis, *Place to Remember*, 21.

peu une famille se forme. Des changements d'attitude entre étudiants deviennent palpables."[50]

- "Our Bossey worship was the catalyst for peace making and for justice seeking both within our small community and as we answered the call to ministry in the wider world."[51]

- "The most important aspect of Bossey was to live and work, pray, dine, study and party with people who daily feared for the physical safety of their families—from hunger (Ethiopia), violence (Brazil), climate change (Tonga Islands) and repression (South Korea)."[52]

- "[T]he real education did not take place in the plenary hall, but around meals in the dining hall, praying together in the chapel, or at late evening parties at Petit Bossey [the student residence], when students shared more personally their own life stories, experiences of church and faith, and hopes for a better world and a more relevant church that would reflect the community that had begun to be realized by these 60 students from 28 different nations and 22 different faith traditions."[53]

The former students's testimonials make strikingly little mention of Bossey's formal courses of study in ecumenism. Instead they more often point to the less formal, extracurricular aspects of life at the Ecumenical Institute as the locus of their transformative experience: the daily round of shared meals, accommodations, worship, and social time. The potentially transformational effect of initially disorienting and ongoing encounters with individuals of a different group toward which an individual is disinclined—observed above in Mezirow's example of ethnocentrism and Taylor's reference to the woman with a negative view of feminists—would appear to also be the phenomenon at work in the experience of some of these Bossey students:

> In an attempt to understand the element of transformation in Bossey's ecumenical education, researchers have identified several contributing components. Not least among them is the fact that students at Bossey live together in a somewhat isolated environment for periods of two intensive weeks for lay seminars, and up

50. Hoegger, *Place to Remember*, 24.
51. Rose, *Place to Remember*, 41.
52. Thomsen, *Place to Remember*, 52.
53. Welsh, *Place to Remember*, 53.

to four months for the Graduate School. Thus their education is around the clock, even at meals, from each other as much as from faculty, and is inevitably intense, both in time and energy, and in the fact that it reaches, and forms, the whole person.[54]

Their sustained encounters with members outside their in-group have the seeming effect of challenging many Bossey students's deep-seated (and presumably negative) beliefs and assumptions about other Christians. These beliefs and assumptions are critically reflected upon and reassessed, and the individual's frame of reference transformed.

From the Classroom, to the Chapel, to 'Dorm Rooms or Pubs'

As one Bossey graduate's testimonial put it, echoing Friere's approach, "In ecumenical education, obtaining experience is more important than transmitting information."[55] The Ecumenical Institute's capacity to bring together individuals from such a broad array of nations and ecclesial traditions is unique. However, its method of placing almost equal emphasis on the curricular and extracurricular dimensions of ecumenical formation is something that can be adapted to other institutions and contexts, potentially to great effect. Robert Kegan, another leading scholar in adult development (who Mezirow cites), notes that, "This kind of learning cannot be accomplished through *in*formational training, the acquisition of skills, but only through *trans*formational education, a 'leading out' from an established habit of mind."[56] In reflecting on how some of his Christian students negotiated the cognitive dissonance they experienced when encountering for the first time a historical-critical reading of the Bible, Philip Tite noted that sometimes "the process is pushed forward most profoundly in dorm rooms or pubs, kicking ideas around in agonizing debates with other students."[57] Similarly, as a Bossey student put it in his testimony above, "[T]he real education did not take place in the plenary hall," but rather in the Ecumenical Institute's chapel, social spaces, dinner tables, and dormitories. A

---

54. Hadsell and Lindner, "Bossey's Ecumenical Formation," 9.
55. Shengjie, *Place to Remember*, 46.
56. Kegan, *Over Our Heads*, 232. Italics in original.
57. Tite, "Necessity of Crisis," 82.

potentially transformational ecumenical ministerial formation, therefore, is one that extends beyond the lecture hall and seminar room.

Much of the literature in the field of ecumenical formation over the past couple of decades stresses the need to ensure that theological students are afforded extracurricular opportunities to engage with other Christian traditions. The Roman Catholic Church's guidelines on ecumenical formation are insistent on this point: "Genuine ecumenical formation must not remain solely academic; it should also include ecumenical experience."[58] The American Protestant ecumenical scholar Michael Kinnamon puts it more plainly still: "While ecumenism needs to be taught in the classroom, it must also be part of the seminary's general life and self-understanding."[59] Within the context of the Ecumenical Institute at Bossey, this dual approach to ecumenical formation is sometimes described as including both "explicit" or "formal" curriculum (e.g. evaluated courses of study consisting of readings, lectures, and assignments) and an "implicit" or "informal" curriculum (e.g. a whole set of experiences that are outside the classroom but which nevertheless have a formative aim).[60] As a former Bossey director put it, such a twofold method acknowledges that, "Church leadership is created not only through academic preparation, but also through dynamic and integrative 'living' experiences."[61]

One of the criticisms sometimes leveled at the ecumenical movement as a whole is that it remains in many ways an academic and institutionally driven exercise finding relatively little tangible expression locally. Even the World Council of Churches acknowledged this critique when participants in the WCC's tenth assembly asserted that the "top-down 'elite' ecumenism of institutions is no longer effective."[62] Therefore, ensuring that ecumenical ministerial formation does not begin and end with lectures and seminars enhances the possibility that practical efforts toward visible unity might result when pastors are actually serving local communities, and that these clergy will be prepared for the on-the-ground ecumenical realities awaiting them:

> Future congregational leaders need to be equipped to translate ecumenical agreements into a local church's pastoral practice

---

58. PCPCU, *Ecumenical Dimension*, §28.
59. Kinnamon, "Ecumenical Formation," 11.
60. Gilligan, "Does What Is Taught," 40.
61. Hadsell, "Two Agendas for Ecumenical Formation," 47.
62. World Council of Churches, *Ecumenical Conversations*, 8.

and spiritual life. Newly ordained ministers will find themselves dealing with ecumenical issues in the parish such as mixed marriages and pastoral issues (i.e. premarital counselling, baptisms, first communion), blended worship opportunities (both community worship events and bilateral with neighboring congregations of other denominations), joint educational opportunities (such as Vacation Bible School and joint youth groups), and shared service opportunities (like Habitat for Humanity, literacy tutoring, and food pantries.).[63]

The Roman Catholic Church has developed the most detailed suggestions on what extracurricular ecumenical opportunities might be offered by a seminary or theological college: organized visits to churches of other traditions, exchanges and joint study days with seminarians of other denominations, guest lecturers from other churches, and occasions for common prayer with other Christians including (but not limited to) the Week of Prayer for Christian Unity.[64] In this same vein Catholic ecumenist Thomas Ryan believes that all ecumenical formation should include "an experiential component, and not be limited to reading books, articles, and dialogue documents, and writing papers."[65] He especially commends participating in common prayer with other Christians and experiencing the liturgical traditions of churches other than one's own.

Ecumenical common prayer is among the most important—and arguably most neglected—aspects of the ecumenical formation of clergy and laity alike. The Second Vatican Council's Decree on Ecumenism notably described prayer for the unity of Christians as "the soul of the whole ecumenical movement."[66] In reflecting on her own vast ecumenical journey, Canadian Catholic ecumenist Catherine Clifford pointed to moments of common prayer with other Christians "as the most formative of all these learning experiences. Thus 'ecumenical formation' can hardly be limited to the experience of intellectual formation."[67] Margaret O'Gara also pointed to moments of common prayer with Christians of other traditions as pivotal in her own ecumenical journey:

---

63. Budde, "Vocation for Unity," 101–2.
64. PCPUC, *Ecumenical Dimension*, §28.
65. Ryan, *Christian Unity*, 134.
66. *Unitatis Redintegratio*, §8.
67. Clifford, "Wake Up Call," 14.

Formation for Transformation

> When we pray together without ceasing for the unity of the church we also hear each other praying. Listening to the prayers of others is a bit like listening to other languages, and of course sometimes we begin to learn the language of our ecumenical partners as well—we learn a second language—and the ear of our heart is opened. This has certainly been my rich experience from praying with my ecumenical colleagues.[68]

As noted above, a number of Bossey graduates have referred to common worship with Christians of other traditions as a key aspect of their ecumenical (trans)formation. In the 1996 survey of American Bossey alumni in particular, "respondents cited worship more frequently than any other factor as the setting for a synthetic and unifying experience that is truly productive of ecumenical consciousness," with the researchers describing the communal worship at Bossey as "the mortar that holds together the bricks of ecumenical formation."[69]

The impact of ecumenical friendships struck up during the course of one's ministerial formation, though difficult to quantify, also merits mention, especially given that interpersonal encounters are frequently mentioned as key factors in the transformation of an individual's frame of reference. There are numerous testimonials to the lasting effect of friendships established between individuals of different church traditions, and the wider impact those relationships can have beyond the individuals immediately involved.

Evangelical theologian and pastor Andrew Draper goes as far as to place a higher premium on ecumenical friendships than on shared worship experiences across Christian traditions: "The litmus test of joining is not how much Communion you have had together or how many services of 'Christian unity' you have participated in but who comes to your children's birthday parties and who you call on when burdened and alone."[70] Another American Protestant, ecumenist Diane Kessler, argues that ecumenical friendships potentially have a kind of multiplier effect because they "provide a strong, safe bond in which people can explore their commonalities, their distinctiveness, and their divisions more deeply, openly, honestly, and safely. These interpersonal encounters can lead to

---

68. O'Gara, *No Turning Back*, 24–25.

69. Erickson and Lindner, "Worship and Prayer," 24.

70. Draper, *Theology of Race and Place*, 289. Draper, following Willie James Jennings, uses "joining" here in the sense of "two unlike bodies in desire for one another becoming one flesh in the body of God."

institutional transformations."⁷¹ O'Gara attests to this, attributing to ecumenical friendships "a theological significance that goes beyond anecdote or sentiment."⁷² As evidence, she relates her own experiences of participation in bilateral ecumenical dialogues, and how friendships developed among individual dialogue participants sometimes resulted in theological breakthroughs between the communions they represented that might not otherwise have been possible. Ryan uses biblical imagery to reflect on these intimate interchurch relationships:

> Ecumenical friendships provide a particularly intense experience of both the desire for unity and the foretaste of unity achieved. Like the disciples on the road to Emmaus, ecumenical friends walk along the road together with Christ as he opens the meaning of the scriptures to them. Because they recognize a common Lord, ecumenical friends recognize one another as his disciples and are again sustained for the long journey ahead.⁷³

American Jesuit theological educator John Ford has observed how a particular course assignment he once designed resulted in not only an acquisition of ecumenical content, but the cultivation of ecumenical friendships. Groups of two to four students, each from a different denomination, were assigned a research topic. Rather than preparing individual papers, the groups were expected to produce a consensus report demonstrating where they had reached agreement on the particular theological or pastoral issue and where further work was still needed:

> For the students, the most valuable aspect of this assignment came from the dynamics of searching together to discover what they held in common and how they could jointly witness their belief by a common statement. In the process the students not only shared their questions and ideas, they also shared their religious convictions and commitment; from this study project emerged a number of cross-denominational friendships which continued after the course had ended. If such interdenominational friendships

---

71. Kessler, "Head Change and Heart Work," 3. To this point I can attest personally. My two closest friends in seminary were not Anglicans, but Presbyterians, and we had predictable theological differences. We remain close friends to this day, meeting annually since our graduation for a week of prayer, study, and fellowship. The impact of those and other ecumenical friendships during my ministerial formation significantly influenced my subsequent vocational commitment to helping reveal the church's visible unity.

72. O'Gara, *No Turning Back*, 37.

73. Ryan, *Christian Unity*, 182.

would become common among students preparing for ministry, ecumenical cooperation would undoubtedly advance much more in the future.[74]

Ryan reflects on this same idea more generally:

> When we get to know each other on a human level, a trust is born that enables us together to broach the most sensitive subjects in a spirit of mutual respect. We are far more influenced by denominational attitudes in our formation than we are willing or able to admit. We have absorbed subtle prejudices toward others. We do not trust each other. And, until we trust, we cannot hear each other.[75]

What each of these observations is pointing toward is the importance of shared experience and shared humanity as a component in developing a deepening awareness of a shared Christian faith. This recognition of a common inheritance of faith between individuals can help contribute to a wider ecclesial recognition between whole communities and institutions.

Transformational Ecumenical Formation

What Mezirow describes as perspective transformation, an ecumenist might borrow biblical and theological language and call conversion—or, continuing with the road to Emmaus story, recognition.[76] It could also be called, to return to the discussion of an earlier chapter, a form of reception, which "involves a recognition of the same faith in another person or community."[77] Each term describes the desired outcome of a holistic approach to ecumenical ministerial formation, one combining both formal or explicit and informal or implicit curricula of the kind modelled in a particularly unique way at Bossey, such that the ecumenical "other"—and the different Christian tradition from which they come—is recognized or received in a way they were not before. The Decree on Ecumenism describes such a "change of heart" as an essential step in one's ecumenical journey.[78] In the same way, a prospective pastor's ecumenical learning "should aim

---

74. Ford, "Ecumenical Commitment," 205.
75. Ryan, *Christian Unity*, 183.
76. See Luke 24:13–35.
77. O'Gara, *No Turning Back*, 32.
78. *Unitatis Redintegratio*, §7.

Transformative Learning

not only to impart cognitive information but also to motivate and enliven the ecumenical conversion and commitment of the participants."[79]

O'Gara used the language of transformation to describe the kind of change of heart she witnessed in her theological students during the course of their studies in ecumenism—a transformation effected through academic learning about other Christian traditions and the ecumenical movement itself, and through experiences of common prayer and fellowship with students of other churches. She described ecumenical formation as a deceivingly innocuous term behind which "stands the reality of conversion and the change that conversion demands."[80] The *Directory*'s section on ecumenical formation was the document's "sleeper," she said. If actually implemented in the manner it outlines, the effect would be "a profound transformation of the Roman Catholic Church."[81]

Thus converted and transformed, the hope and vision therefore is that the student (Roman Catholic or otherwise) who emerges from the kind of holistic ecumenical ministerial formation outlined above is one who will manifest an "authentically ecumenical disposition,"[82] and who will seek to work across denominational boundaries at every turn in their respective ministries, "with the learning outcome that all aspects of ministry and leadership will be undertaken ecumenically."[83] Mezirow might readily recognize the desired result that O'Gara is describing as a successful perspective transformation.

The objective of ecumenical ministerial formation, therefore, is not only the acquisition of knowledge about and creating awareness of ecumenism, but rather nothing less than transformation, conversion. The goal is "not to create another separate discipline of accumulated knowledge and specialized information, but [to be] understood as a *qualitative* dimension of all theological education, i.e. that all theological disciplines should enable students to become active participants in the ecumenical movement."[84] In the same way Freire's "education for freedom"[85] was intended to liberate Latin America's disenfranchised citizens as full participants in their lives

---

79. PCPCU, *Ecumenical Dimension*, §7(a)
80. O'Gara, "Formation for Transformation," 26.
81. O'Gara, "Formation for Transformation," 26.
82. PCPCU, *Directory*, §70.
83. World Council of Churches, *Ecumenical Conversations*, 42.
84. Werner, "Ecumenical Formation," 105. Emphasis in original.
85. Graham, et al., *Theological Reflection*, 182.

and that of their country, ecumenical "formation for transformation"[86] is intended to create the conditions for "personal 'heart changes'"[87] that will make ecumenical engagement for those so transformed a fundamental aspect of their Christian discipleship.

To what extent do the conditions for such transformational ecumenical learning currently exist within the seminaries, theological colleges, and other centers of ministerial formation of the Anglican Church of Canada? What is the experience of those who have received their ministerial formation in those institutions, and to what extent are they aware of and committed to the ecumenical movement as a result of their ministerial formation? These questions will be explored in the next chapter.

---

86. O'Gara, "Formation for Transformation," 23.
87. Kessler, "Heart Change and Head Work," 4.

4

Surveying Canadian Anglican Ecumenical Formation

IF AN ECUMENICAL CONSCIOUSNESS and a disposition to work ecumenically is to be inculcated in members of the clergy, their ministerial formation must intentionally include ecumenical content, both curricular and extracurricular (or, in the language used to describe the Ecumenical Institute at Bossey's approach, explicit or formal and implicit or informal). The extent of agreement on this principle is perhaps most clearly expressed in the work of the Joint Working Group between the Roman Catholic Church and World Council of Churches, which includes in two of its reports specific recommendations on the shape and content of ecumenical formation for clergy, the details of which are outlined in a previous chapter and will be revisited below.

The degree to which these and similar recommendations with respect to ecumenical ministerial formation have ever been implemented has rarely been measured, at least not in Canada. In 1998 the Canadian Centre for Ecumenism sponsored a survey "to examine the state of ecumenical education in Canada in terms of how ecumenism is being 'taught' in theological faculties and institutes around the country."[1] Among other things that study revealed that only two of twenty-three institutions responding offered a specific course in ecumenism, neither compulsory. While "significant ecumenical content" was identified in the curricula of some of the respondents, especially in courses on church

---

1. Dowd, "Ecumenical Education in Canada," 24.

history, ecclesiology, and systematic theology, this was the case for fewer than half of the institutions surveyed.

The explanation most frequently offered for this paucity of ecumenical curricular content was a lack of capacity: "[M]any institutes reported that, while they would like to 'do' more in this area, there simply were not the resources to accomplish the task."[2] The survey also asked about extracurricular ecumenical content: "To supplement the academic activity of your institute or faculty, do you sponsor extra-academic opportunities (ecumenical prayer, liturgy, social activities, fraternal exchanges, etc.)?" Of the twenty-three responses received, "few institutes did very many of these things, perhaps one or two activities sufficing for the most part."[3] When specifically asked about their observance of the Week of Prayer for Christian Unity, "Of the twenty-three respondents, eleven simply answered, 'No,' a disappointing fifty percent!"[4]

The 1998 survey was revealing in many ways, given that it appears to be the first (and seemingly only) attempt to assess the landscape of ecumenical formation in Canada's institutions of theological education. While Dowd acknowledged the limits of the conclusions that could be drawn from his survey, which he described as a "brief exposé," he did suggest that its results were a confirmation that, "The ecumenical movement is still young in the life of the church, and as such is not fully diffused into the practical life of the denominations (or their theological colleges)."[5] Put another way, the study revealed an evident lack of ecumenical reception, particularly in the preparation of candidates for ordained ministry.

That survey provides some helpful background, although there are limits to its application for this research. In addition to being twenty years old, Dowd's study was not specifically aimed at Anglican theological faculties, colleges, or seminaries. Since the focus of this research is the current ecumenical engagement of the Anglican Church of Canada, and specifically of its clergy, a new and still more targeted survey was in order.

Such a survey was one of two undertaken as a part of this research. One (which will be explored later in this chapter) focuses on the ecumenical experience of individual Canadian Anglican clergy both during and after their formal ministerial formation. Another—to which we will first

2. Dowd, "Ecumenical Education in Canada," 27.
3. Dowd, "Ecumenical Education in Canada," 26.
4. Dowd, "Ecumenical Education in Canada," 27.
5. Dowd, "Ecumenical Education in Canada," 27.

turn our attention—surveyed theological colleges, seminaries, and other centers for ministerial formation recognized as having a formal affiliation with the Anglican Church of Canada.

A Survey of Canadian Anglican Seminaries and Theological Colleges

At the time of the survey, fifteen institutions were identified as centers currently active and primarily engaged in the training and preparation of candidates for ordination in the Anglican Church of Canada, as listed in the section entitled "Universities, Colleges, and Theological Colleges Associated with the Anglican Church of Canada" in the most recent edition of the *Anglican Church Directory*. These included residential seminaries and theological colleges as well as some diocesan-based schools for ministry that primarily operate on a distance model of education.

The online survey consisted of seventeen closed- and open-ended questions and was sent as a link embedded in an introductory email to the identifiable heads of each institution explaining the purpose of the research and inviting them to complete the survey themselves or to designate a suitable individual within their organization to do so. Deliberately, some of the questions closely matched the wording of some of those from Dowd's 1998 survey, so as to allow the possibility of at least some comparison. Of the fifteen institutions solicited, ten completed the online survey, representing a response rate of a little more than 66 percent. The institutions that took part in the survey were:[6]

- Arthur Turner Training School (Iqaluit, NU)
- Atlantic School of Theology (Halifax, NS)
- College of Emmanuel and St. Chad (Saskatoon, SK)
- Huron College (London, ON)
- Montreal Diocesan Theological College (Montreal, QC)
- Queen's College (St. John's, NL)
- St. Paul University (Ottawa, ON)
- Trinity College (Toronto, ON)

---

6. The respondents were not obliged by the survey to identify themselves or their institutions, but each nevertheless volunteered to do so.

- Vancouver School of Theology (Vancouver, BC)
- Wycliffe College (Toronto, ON)

Although approximately one-third of the institutions sought out for participation in the survey did not respond to the invitation, the theological colleges and seminaries with the largest student bodies and faculties in the country are among the respondents. Indeed, the respondents include every Anglican-associated institution offering the master of divinity degree in the country, all but one of which was (at the time of the survey) an accredited member of the Association of Theological Schools in the United States and Canada.[7] This means that the participating institutions collectively include in their student bodies almost every Canadian Anglican pursuing the traditional, three-year path to ordination at the time of the survey. Also significant is that each major region of Canada, including the Far North, is represented in the sample.

In addition to indicating which region of the country in which their institution was situated, respondents were also asked to describe their institution's organizational model. The choices were based on the categories examined in chapter four.

Five (50 percent) described themselves as part of an ecumenical federation or consortium, an arrangement by which their institution exists in a formal relationship with institutions of other Christian traditions while maintaining a distinct Anglican identity and degree of autonomy. Three respondents (30 percent) indicated they form part of a single organically merged institution in which different Christian traditions, including Anglicanism, are represented. One institution described itself as a "stand alone" school without any formal affiliations to any other entities or Christian traditions. One respondent indicated that their institution did not fit exclusively into any of the other three categories, explaining that though it is an historically Anglican school federated with colleges of other Christian traditions, Anglicans in fact today represent a minority in its student body.

Each respondent was also asked to describe the primary teaching (or delivery) method of their institution. Eight of the respondents (80 percent) replied that their institutions were primarily residential, with full- or

---

7. In North America, the master of divinity (MDiv) degree has been the standard accredited form of ministerial formation, typically delivered as a full-time, residential program over three years. All but one of the ten responding institutions in this survey offer a master of divinity program.

part-time students physically attending classes on campus.[8] One described its method as locally based, as in a diocesan school for ministry unaffiliated with an academic institution, such as a university faculty of theology. The remaining respondent described the primary teaching design of their institution as a mix of residential, locally based, and distance education.

The other questions asked in the survey were largely based on recommendations and goals for the ecumenical formation of future clergy articulated in documents produced by various bodies: the World Council of Churches, the Roman Catholic Church (and the two working together through the Joint Working Group), the Anglican Church of Canada, and the Anglican Communion. Highlights of these documents and their recommendations were presented in an earlier chapter, and they make many of the same suggestions for ecumenical ministerial formation in terms of curriculum, worship, and extracurricular activities.

In its ninth report, in a section entitled "Ecumenical Formation: A Key to Ecumenical Reception," the Joint Working Group between the Roman Catholic Church and the World Council of Churches makes the following statement: "Ecumenical formation must be an essential element for candidates for ordained ministry."[9] Respondents to the survey we asked if they agreed with the JWG's unequivocal assertion. All said they were in agreement, and each offered an elaboration when invited to explain their initial response:

- "Familiarity with the range of Christian expressions is necessary for effective engagement with Canadian society, and to respond the contemporary challenges confronting Christianity in the global North."

- "I agree for theological reasons: in particular, our message of reconciliation through Christ is compromised by Christian division and denominational silos."

- "In a global context and the multi-faith/multi-ethnic reality that is Canada, ecumenical awareness and capacity for dialogue and collaboration is vital. Without it, clergy and their congregations are limited in their effectiveness."

---

8. At the same time five of these eight institutions also offer what the Association of Theological Schools defines as "comprehensive distance education," the implications of which will be discussed in a subsequent chapter.

9. Joint Working Group, *Ninth Report*, §143.

- "In the modern world, those connected with churches expect ecumenical and collaborative ministries. The demographics of churches necessitate collaborations in sharing resources and ministries. Such collaborations require informed leadership."

- "'So that they may all be one . . . that the world may believe.' Because our relationships with other Christians is part of our witness to the world. And practically, working together is the way of the future so we should learn a bit about each other and start modeling that early on."

- "First, the student body of the school is ecumenical in makeup, requiring ecumenical engagement and learning from the outset. Second, Christian denominations cannot respond to, or live out, the mission of Christ in isolation. Third, people are becoming less likely to participate in church life simply out of a sense of denominational identity. Finally, I believe that we are call by Christ to unity."

- "Ordained leaders have a responsibility to teach and to live out the ecumenical commitments of the Anglican Church of Canada. Members of the Anglican Church of Canada, in various ways, live in an ecumenical (not to mention interfaith) world. Their own lived experience of ecumenism (e.g., inter-church marriages, ecumenical justice coalitions, etc.) needs to be supported and informed by their leaders. Christians need to recognize and claim their common faith in order to bear effective witness in a secular culture. None can ignore the Lord's own prayer that all be one."

- "Any adequate theology of the Church must seek to understand the Church in its different expressions."

- "It is firstly a theological imperative (Jesus' prayer that his church be one), but also pragmatically it is a necessity for mutual support and cooperation in our increasingly post-Christian culture."

- "Preparation for ordained ministry requires the broadest possible exposure to partners, resources, and a definitional framework for what that ministry will look like. To exclude ecumenical formation would be inherently self-limiting."

The remainder of the survey's questions attempt to measure the degree to which these institutions's fulsome endorsement of the essential nature of ecumenical ministerial formation is actually reflected in their curricula, faculty, worship, and extracurricular offerings.

Curriculum

With respect to the formal courses of study for future clergy, the Joint Working Group's most recent report (2013) makes two specific recommendations: (1) Seminaries and theological colleges should offer a specific course on ecumenism with a detailed curriculum; and (2) every other field of theology should include an ecumenical dimension. "Both," states the report, "are part of ecumenical formation, so that ecumenism is not seen as an isolated speciality, but exists as a living component in all theological discourse."[10]

Only one of the ten respondents reported that their curriculum for candidates for ministry included a compulsory course in ecumenism. Called "Ecclesiology in an Ecumenical Age," the brief course description reads: "The church as a sign of communion and salvation in service of the human community. Catholic ecclesial self-understanding, the unity of the Christian churches, structuring of ministries, the laity, and diversity of life within a world church." This institution offers a second ecumenically oriented course as an elective: "Anglicans and Unity," described as "a study of ecumenical issues in Anglican history, in the work of major theologians, in contemporary ecumenical dialogues; the pastoral implications of full communion and interim agreements with ecumenical partners."[11]

Four other respondents indicated that their institution also offered an elective with an ecumenical theme, but no required course. Of these four, two are offered exclusively online, one through a partner college of another tradition, and one is a special seminar offered annually during the Week of Prayer for Christian Unity. Interestingly, without prompting, some of the respondents whose institutions do not offer a compulsory ecumenics course sought to justify this reality by insisting that ecumenical awareness among their students is cultivated by other means. So they may not insist on or even offer an explicit course on ecumenism,

- "... but our program structure requires students to enroll in courses in other denominational colleges."
- "... but ecumenical resources are used in the theology and pastoral practice courses, as well as formation programs, on a regular basis."
- "... but an ecumenical focus pervades what is taught."

10. Joint Working Group, *Ninth Report*, §143. The Roman Catholic Church's directives in this respect go even further, insisting that a core course on ecumenism be compulsory for its seminarians.

11. Saint Paul University, "Master of Divinity."

- "... but there are a variety of courses that discuss different ecclesial approaches to theology and ministry."
- "... though I try to incorporate the ecumenical documents into formation on Anglicanism."

Others responded that,

- "Most of our ecumenical formation happens as students engage with one another."
- "Ecumenism is embedded in the curriculum."
- "... this subject is in the area of responsibility of our United Church partner!"

Two respondents went further still, questioning the need for such courses:

- "In my experience, ecumenical theology is not taught. We have a great tradition and no shortage of ecumenical theology and ecumenical reflection in the twentieth century but we rarely bring these documents (e.g. *Baptism, Eucharist and Ministry*; *Mission and Evangelism: An Ecumenical Affirmation*) into the classroom. I think it would be hard to interest students to sign up for a class called "ecumenical theology"—they just do ecumenism, they don't want to think about it. But it's important to think about and we have great resources to help us do so. The challenge is incorporating those resources in new ways into material we already teach. The other challenge is the narrowness of our ecumenism. Often it's only mainline, liberal denominations. This has at least two problems. First, it misses the great tradition of ecumenical reflection present in something like the Lausanne Movement (which also has its own helpful documents). Second, it misses the nature of the new Pentecost in our midst and the pentecostal, diasporic churches that are part of our communities but which are not on our horizon in any meaningful way."
- "I think we are past courses which extol the virtues of ecumenism. We conduct classes in which students present are from multiple denominations and course readings and lectures cover topics in an ecumenical fashion."

With respect to the Joint Working Group's second recommendation about curriculum—that there should be an ecumenical dimension to the teaching of every field of theology—the survey asked: "Please list the courses, seminars, workshops, etc., offered by your institution which include an ecumenical dimension. (For example, are courses in such disciplines as systematic theology, ecclesiology, or church history taught from the perspective of a single Christian tradition or approached from different ecclesial perspectives?)" The respondents's replies in this area were more in line with the hopes expressed by the Joint Working Group, with all ten institutions indicating that at least some of the courses offered in the various theological disciplines included some ecumenical content. Four were specific about which courses offered this dimension, naming classes on mission, liturgy, sacraments, pastoral theology, doctrine, preaching, Christian formation, church history, theology, Bible, ethics, and one course introducing students to "theological praxis in the context of exploring the church, the faith, and our place in the world." The other six respondents were more general in their answers:

- "We no longer list courses as having only an Anglican focus."
- "The material is taught from an Anglican perspective, but we use Roman Catholic and other non-Anglican Protestant sources. In systematic theology, for example, an attempt is made to understand other Christian streams, including Roman Catholic, liberal Protestant, evangelical, etc."
- "Ninety percent of our courses are ecumenical in the sense of engaging multiple Christian traditions and voices in the readings, research, and discussions."
- "Virtually all of these courses are taught with an ecumenical perspective."
- "Virtually every course we offer . . . has intentional and 'environmental' ecumenical dimensions."
- "All our courses are taught ecumenically."

While the survey did not ask about for a detailed description of any ecumenical course content, it did request respondents to "list any ecumenical agreed statements, guidelines, documents, etc., included in the curriculum or readings lists of courses, seminars, workshops, etc., offered by your institution." The only such texts listed by more than one institution were *Baptism, Eucharist and Ministry*, reports of the Anglican-Roman Catholic International Commission, and the Waterloo Declaration, the principle text of the full communion agreement between the Anglican Church of Canada and the Evangelical Lutheran Church in Canada.

The question of *who* does the teaching was also raised in the survey. While the Joint Working Group's recommendations do not explicitly suggest that theological faculty and lecturers ought to come from a variety of Christian traditions, the Roman Catholic Church's guidelines for ecumenical formation do, as do other ecumenical scholars with direct and extensive experience in ecumenical formation.[12] All but one (90 percent) of the survey respondents indicated that some of their teaching staff includes individuals from Christian traditions other than Anglicanism. A similar question was asked with respect to the denominational composition of the institution's student bodies, since ecumenical scholars and teachers like Mitzi Budde have observed that such variety can, in and of itself, have a positive impact: "A seminary with an ecumenically diverse student body offers an environment which can be a rich encounter with other ways of talk about and to God."[13] The Joint Working Group has described undergoing ministerial formation for students of other Christian traditions as "one of the most fundamental learning experiences."[14] This has already been observed in a concrete way through the potential effects of a highly diverse student body at the Ecumenical Institute at Bossey. When asked, "Does your institution's student body include individuals from Christian traditions other than Anglicanism?" seven of the institutions replied positively (70 percent), two negatively (20 percent), and one did not indicate either way.

Interestingly, one of the colleges participating in this survey has a majority of students who are not Anglican. Sixty percent of students enrolled at Wycliffe College in Toronto come from other, mostly evangelical, churches or denominations. The college actively courts students from "a broad evangelical constituency,"[15] and currently brands itself as "an evangelical graduate school of theology rooted in the Anglican tradition."

---

12. PCPCU, *Ecumenical Dimension*, §20(d). See also Budde, "Vocation for Unity," 103–4; and Ryan, *Christian Unity*, 134.

13. Budde, "Vocation for Unity," 101.

14. Joint Working Group, *Seventh Report*, 17 (§4).

15. Gardner, "Challenges Draw Trinity and Wycliffe Closer," 3.

Field Education

All of the responding institutions indicated that they offered some form of field education for students preparing for ordination. When asked what, if any, ecumenical component such field education includes, most (60 percent) indicated that this was largely dependent upon the ministry context of their placement and/or their field supervisor. As one respondent put it, "The ecumenical dimension is found in the experience of students as it arises from the particulars of their placement." Therefore, if a student is placed in a field placement with a congregation and/or supervisor with a high level of ecumenical engagement, then this would likely be reflected in the student's field education experience. Examples offered of what such ecumenical components might resemble included participation in gatherings of local interdenominational ministerial associations and chaplaincy in health care facilities.

Two respondents (20 percent) revealed that it is in fact possible for Anglican students in their institutions to complete a field placement in a worshipping community of another tradition. One theological college indicated that one of their students was in the process of completing a field placement in a congregation of the Evangelical Lutheran Church in Canada (a denomination in full communion with the Anglican Church of Canada). Another stated that while it requires Anglican students to complete two terms of field education in a church of their own tradition, an additional term could be added "for those who either want further study in that same placement or for those who would like an opportunity to experience a different denomination or religion." Two respondents (20 percent) said that their institutions's field education program does not take ecumenism into account.

Extracurricular Activities

Chapter two observed how advocates of ecumenical formation emphasize the need for a holistic approach, stressing the importance of creating extra-academic ecumenical experiences alongside teaching formal courses in ecumenics and providing an ecumenical dimension to other theological disciplines. American ecumenist Michael Kinnamon's observation bears repeating: "While ecumenism needs to be taught in the classroom, it must also be part of the seminary's general life and self-understanding."[16] As

---

16. Kinnamon, "Ecumenical Formation," 11.

noted earlier, the Roman Catholic document, *The Ecumenical Dimension in the Formation of Those Engaged in Pastoral Work*, furnishes the most detailed suggestions on what extracurricular ecumenical opportunities might be offered by a seminary or theological college: organized visits to churches of other traditions, exchanges and joint study days with seminarians of other denominations, guest lecturers from other churches, and occasions for common prayer with other Christians including (but not limited to) the Week of Prayer for Christian Unity.[17]

Two questions related to extra-academic ecumenical initiatives were therefore posed to the institutions surveyed. The first asked, "What extracurricular ecumenical activities (e.g. prayer, social activities, exchanges, etc.) does your institution organize or sponsor?" All ten respondents (100 percent) indicated that some form of extracurricular ecumenical activity involving students does take place. One simply stated, without elucidation, that it was "a very long list" of activities, while another explained that "we have a good rapport with the [local] Catholic priest and bishop."

The remaining eight respondents stated that for the most part extracurricular ecumenical activities involved some form of prayer. For example:

- "Weekly ecumenical evening prayer."
- "Our consortium holds monthly times of shared worship followed by a meal."
- "Orientation happens together."
- "Worship and meals with other ecumenical institutions in our consortium."
- "Chapel is ecumenical and requires students from a variety of Christian traditions to work together in worship."
- "Weekly 'ecumenical vespers'—service led alternately by Roman Catholics, Anglicans, and Orthodox Christians."

Only two respondents (20 percent) clearly identified extra-academic ecumenical activities that did not involve liturgy or some kind of shared meal. One mentioned "student-led social events" and another a "shared food collection project" for a local food bank.

The second related question asked specifically if the respondent's institution observed the Week of Prayer for Christian Unity. Nine respondents

---

17. PCPCU, *Ecumenical Dimension*, §28.

(90 percent) indicated that this annual observance dedicated to praying for the church's visible unity, which dates back to 1908, is in some way marked in their institutions. For instance:

- "We have a joint service with the Catholic seminary."
- "We invite leaders from as many of the churches to which the student body belong to participate."
- "At the school it forms the basic focus for that week's chapel liturgies. We usually have a speaker who will focus on the theme at our Wednesday community gathering."
- "Guest preachers for each day; social gathering with guests each day."

Ecumenism: More or Less of a Priority?

The survey concluded by asking respondents a broad, open-ended question regarding the development over time of their college or seminary's overall ecumenical orientation: "Has ecumenism become more or less of a priority or important value for your institution in the past twenty years? Can you explain how and why?"[18]

Most of those completing the survey did not respond with unqualified "more" or "less" answers, but instead offered nuanced replies. Four respondents reported that as their student body has grown more ecumenically diverse, their institution's orientation has by necessity grown more ecumenical also:

- "We are seeing a growing number of non-Anglican students come to the college, so we have to adapt our courses and be more intentional about meeting the needs of the non-Anglican judicatories."
- "It is part of the DNA of our institution. It has been expanding to denominations beyond our traditional three—Presbyterian, United, and Anglican. Lately we also get students from Lutheran, Mennonite, and a variety of non-mainline churches."

---

18. The frame of twenty years was chosen because that is the amount of time that had passed since Dowd's survey for the Canadian Centre for Ecumenism was conducted. It also roughly represents the passage of a generation.

- "Part of this [increase in students from other Christian traditions] is the result of economic necessity and the lack of other local options for those in non-Anglican and non-Roman Catholic traditions."
- "Major expansion to students from other denominations. . . . Our college could not have survived with only the recruitment base of 20 years ago."

One respondent described ecumenism in his small institution as having shifted over time from being a priority to nothing less than "a necessary basis for survival." He said this has been expressed in the manner in which all three denominational partners of that particular consortium of colleges "has had the experience of being 'carried' by the whole partnership during a time of crisis." This institutional experience, he said, has had an impact on the ecumenical formation of individuals preparing for the current context of ministry: "There is a consciousness that our shared work [as denominational colleges] models the reality of the ministry for which we are equipping students, where no one church or tradition has all the resources needed for mission and ministry, especially in the small congregations and communities which are our focus." Interestingly, the principal of a much larger theological college made a similar observation: "There is also the ecclesial reality that mainline churches are in steep numerical decline. Church closures change the nature of ecumenical relationships in the community, and it is important that our students have an understanding of different ecclesial traditions if they are to cooperate with or minister effectively to people outside their traditions."

Observations and Analysis

The data provided by the individual respondents is similar enough that some general observations can be made and an overall portrait at least sketched out. Most Canadian Anglican centers of ministerial formation exist within historically ecumenical structures, such as interdenominational federations, consortia, or organically merged institutions. The majority of instruction is offered on a residential basis, meaning that students are required to be physically present on campus for at least a significant portion of their ministerial formation. Most have ecumenically diverse faculty and student bodies, or form a part of a larger grouping of non-Anglican institutions that provides that variety. While there is unanimity that ecumenical

Surveying Canadian Anglican Ecumenical Formation

formation is an essential element for individuals preparing for ordained ministry, almost none has a required course in ecumenism for its master of divinity students; a few others offer an optional course. Ecumenical documents are only occasionally included in course reading lists, and those that are used tend to be relatively dated. Most courses in other theological disciplines include at least some reference to non-Anglican sources. All institutions have a field placement component to their ministerial formation, but determining if that experience includes any ecumenical dimension seems to rest almost entirely with the student. There are occasions for extracurricular ecumenical activities, and these tend to be centered on occasional common prayer and shared meals. The Week of Prayer for Christian Unity is universally observed in some fashion.

When examined against Dowd's 1998 survey of theological faculties and institutes, there appear to be some signs of improvement, acknowledging that there are limits to what can be compared since his survey extended beyond Anglican centers of ministerial formation. For example, all of the respondents to the 2018 survey indicated that they in some way commemorate the Week of Prayer for Christian Unity, compared to fewer than half in the 1998 study. Similarly, in 2018 there was at least one compulsory course in ecumenics (a "fairly self-contained field of enquiry" defined as "a unique body of material and insight produced by the modern ecumenical movement"[19]) being taught in Canada, whereas twenty years earlier there was apparently none.

That being said, the results of the 2018 survey make plain that in most Anglican institutions of ministerial formation in Canada, ecumenism is not being explicitly taught. It is worth reviewing again the reasons for this that the respondents offered above. They can be summarized as follows:

- The existing program structure requires Anglican students to enroll in courses offered by other denominational colleges;
- Most other courses include some ecumenical perspective, rendering an explicit course in ecumenism unnecessary;
- Ecumenical formation occurs organically as students of different traditions engage with each other;

---

19. Martensen, *Teaching of Ecumenics*, xxi.

- The existing curriculum for ministerial formation is already at capacity, and ecumenism would have to be incorporated into the material already being taught;
- Students would not be interested in an explicit course on ecumenism.

These reasons are not new and have come under the judgement of ecumenists before. For example, it is notable the extent to which these explanations from Anglican institutions resemble those offered by Roman Catholic seminaries or theology faculties also choosing not to offer a core course in ecumenism, as critiqued by Clifford in an earlier chapter.

Such reasoning has also been challenged at the global level of the ecumenical movement. In 1986 the World Council of Churches organized an international workshop on the teaching of ecumenics at, fittingly, the Ecumenical Institute at Bossey. The event gathered more than fifty ecumenists, teachers, and scholars from around the world for ten days of conversations. An anthology of papers presented at the gathering was published the following year, and was intended to serve as a kind of handbook for teachers of ecumenism. The volume's introduction, written by American Lutheran theologian and ecumenist Daniel Martensen, reads at times like a *crie de cœur* on what was the current state of ecumenical ministerial formation:

> The traditional encyclopedia of theological seminary concerns tends to more than fill the available space in a given curriculum, as most curricula are presently organized. Ecumenics as a self-conscious field of enquiry sits uneasily on the periphery of late twentieth-century Christian theological education. People committed to the teaching of ecumenics experience along with the uneasiness a sense of urgency, urgency related to the crying need for maintaining a corporate ecumenical memory. After nearly seventy years of organized ecumenical effort, we have no systematic means of transmitting experience, knowledge and vision generated in those decades.[20]

Such a systematic means of ecumenical transmission remains elusive more than twenty years later, and so this plea for ecumenics to be accorded as permanent a place in the curricula of seminaries and colleges as other theological disciplines resonates as much as ever. For example, Mitzi J. Budde, herself a teacher of ecumenics at a U.S. seminary, more recently noted that while divinity students are often taught the history of the church's

20. Martensen, *Teaching of Ecumenics*, ix.

divisions—heresies, schisms, and contemporary denominationalism—rarely are they instructed in the ecumenical movement's decades of efforts to reconcile and heal these historic breaches in the church. The result: "We re-inculcate the divisions of the church into every successive generation."[21]

More than one respondent to the 2018 survey of institutions suggested that a discrete course in ecumenism is unnecessary because the fact that a seminary or theological college exists within a multidenominational organization of some kind ensures, as if by some form of osmosis, the development of an ecumenical consciousness among its students. As one response to the questionnaire put it, "Most of our ecumenical formation happens as students engage with one another." Martensen challenges this claim: "Experience in theological consortia or other cooperative ventures in theological education clearly demonstrates that there is no automatic ecumenical gain from cross-registration among different seminaries, or even in attending a 'non-denominational' or 'ecumenical' theological school."[22]

Indeed, neither is there any guarantee that opportunities for such ecumenical cross-registrations will be taken up by students. For example, when the Toronto School of Theology was established in 1970 (see chapter 2), one of its unique ecumenical attributes was that students were not only free, but actively encouraged, to take advantage of the Christian diversity represented in the TST's seven member schools and enroll in courses outside of their home college. TST students initially took this up with zeal, with 96 percent of them taking at least one course in another college in the new consortium's first year.[23] In subsequent decades that trend has undergone a "dramatic (and disappointing) change from TST's early years,"[24] as the following chart illustrates.

---

21. Budde, "Vocation for Unity," 98.
22. Martensen, *Teaching of Ecumenics*, xii.
23. Hayes, "Toronto School of Theology."
24. Hayes, "Toronto School of Theology."

Table 2: Percentage of TST basic degree students staying in home college[25]

College	1977–78	2015–16
Emmanuel (United)	57	96
Knox (Presbyterian)	55	86
Regis (Catholic)	53	65
St. Augustine's (Catholic)	29	97
St. Michael's (Catholic)	43	76
Trinity (Anglican)	43	81
Wycliffe (Anglican)	45	90

So, for example, while more than half of Wycliffe College students were taking at least one course at another TST institution in 1977–78, that number had plummeted to 10 percent by the 2015–16 academic year.

Alan Hayes, a professor of church history at Wycliffe and the Toronto School of Theology's director between 2007 and 2018, admits that, "From this point of view, TST has fallen short of its ecumenical potential; it appears that the exposure of students to points of view outside the tradition of their college registration has declined significantly."[26] The reasons for this dearth of cross-registrations have not been ascertained by the TST, although Hayes nevertheless postulates some possible explanations:

- Ecumenical zeal in general has waned since the years immediately after Vatican II;
- There are broader cultural signs—for instance, in the political realm—that people prefer to listen to points of view they agree with, and avoid others;

---

25. "Basic degree students" includes those pursuing an MDiv, and also those registered in the master of religious education, master of theological studies, master of pastoral studies, master of sacred music, and master of arts in ministry and spirituality programs.

26. Hayes, "Toronto School of Theology."

- Declining church memberships may have inclined denominational mentalities to turn inward;
- After the first generation of TST college leaders, who pioneered TST together and built up a warm personal chemistry, the second generation began to return to a "business-as-usual," self-protective attitude;
- For various reasons, degree requirements increased, and many could only be met by courses offered in the student's home college;
- The number of part-time commuting students increased, putting scheduling pressure on a few premium time slots from Tuesday to Thursday, which colleges filled with required courses. Students therefore had less opportunity to choose electives outside their college;
- Since TST has a system for transferring some funding to colleges in proportion to the number of students they teach, college leaders have a financial incentive to keep their students in their own college.[27]

Some of these explanations will be taken up later, when I propose a revised approach to ecumenical ministerial formation. It is sufficient for the moment to observe that the TST's own cross-registration statistics demonstrate that even in an organization that proudly describes itself as "one of the largest ecumenical centers for theological education in the English-speaking world," representing "dozens of denominations and diverse theological and cultural traditions, creating unusually rich opportunities for theological conversation,"[28] there is no guarantee that many students will take advantage of those rich opportunities. Nor can the kind of structural diversity that characterizes the TST in and of itself ensure the kind of lasting cross-pollination of students and courses envisioned by the consortium's founders.

Neither can an "ecumenical gain" be assumed to have been achieved through simply offering other traditions's perspectives in the teaching of other theological disciplines, such as church history, systematic theology, or ethics. "[U]nless ecumenics is taught in a self-conscious fashion," Martensen concludes, "it will not be taught at all," and the result risks being an irretrievable loss of the ecumenical movement's past achievements and of "the ecumenical vision of the future."[29] Budde points out that whatever

27. Hayes, "Toronto School of Theology."
28. Toronto School of Theology, "Why TST?"
29. Martensen, *Teaching of Ecumenics*, xii.

a theological college's claims about its ecumenical commitment, content, or ethos, "every aspect of the seminary experience teaches," including that which is absent from the curriculum or extracurricular life: "Ultimately, every component speaks about what the institutional community values, believes, and confesses."[30]

The survey's data reveals in a quantifiable way that the overwhelming majority of those preparing for ordination to the priesthood in the Anglican Church of Canada do not receive any explicit ecumenical formation during their time in seminary or theological college, at least not in the form of a dedicated course in ecumenics. The data also suggests, however, that students at most of these institutions are presented with at least the potential for ecumenical engagement of some kind. Sometimes this is through encounters of various kinds with faculty and/or fellow students from other denominations, through exposure to another Christian tradition's approach to a discipline like theological ethics or biblical studies, or by experiencing worship according to the rites of another church.

Is this sufficient to inculcate the kind of "authentically ecumenical disposition,"[31] envisioned by those who argue for a more robust expression of ecumenical ministerial formation in seminaries and theological colleges? Will it cultivate clergy who will seek to work across denominational boundaries at every turn in their respective ministries, "with the learning outcome that all aspects of ministry and leadership will be undertaken ecumenically"?[32] Attempting to ascertain this necessitates another line of inquiry, this one directed at Canadian Anglican clergy themselves.

A Survey of Canadian Anglican Deacons, Priests, and Bishops

The second survey conducted in relation to this research targeted ordained clergy of the Anglican Church of Canada and their experience of ecumenical formation. It also sought to elicit examples of any ecumenical dimensions to their current ministry contexts. This too was an online survey, consisting of 30 closed- and open-ended questions. Since there exists no single digital distribution network for all Canadian Anglican clergy, an introductory email, which included a link to the online survey, was sent to each of the

30. Budde, "Vocation for Unity," 103.
31. PCPCU, *Directory*, §70.
32. World Council of Churches, *Ecumenical Conversations*, 42.

Surveying Canadian Anglican Ecumenical Formation

church's 29 other diocesan bishops, as well as to the Bishop Ordinary of the Canadian Armed Forces. The bishops were invited to complete the surveys themselves and to distribute it through their own networks to clergy under their oversight.

A total of 206 ordained individuals from twenty five dioceses and the Anglican Military Ordinariate completed the survey. In terms of formal jurisdictions within the Anglican Church of Canada, this represents a response rate of just over 78 percent. With respect to individuals, a clearly definable response rate is difficult to establish, since there is no reliable way of accurately ascertaining exactly how many clergy may have received the survey through their bishop. Nevertheless, the two hundred and six responses received represent a useful sample, not least because nearly every region of the country is represented among the respondents, spread reasonably evenly among the church's four ecclesiastical provinces.[33]

The vast majority of those replying (84 percent) were priests, although seventeen deacons and sixteen bishops[34] also participated in the survey (each of those orders representing 8 percent of the total responses). Nearly three-quarters of respondents (72 percent) described the primary context of their ministry as "congregational," with more than half (60 percent) indicating that they were serving in ministry on a full-time stipendiary basis. The remainder were serving on a part-time basis, as volunteers, or were retired.

---

33. As the name makes plain, the Ecclesiastical Province of British Columbia and Yukon encompasses the five dioceses present in that civil province and territory (British Columbia, Caledonia, Kootenay, New Westminster, Territory of the People, and Yukon). The Ecclesiastical Province of Rupert's Land includes ten dioceses spanning the Prairies and the North (Arctic, Athabasca, Brandon, Calgary, Edmonton, Mishamikoweesh, Qu'Appelle, Rupert's Land, Saskatchewan, and Saskatoon). The Ecclesiastical Province of Ontario contains seven dioceses present in that civil province (Algoma, Huron, Moosonee, Niagara, Ontario, Ottawa, and Toronto). The Ecclesiastical Province of Canada, despite its historic name, gathers but the country's seven easternmost dioceses (Central Newfoundland, Eastern Newfoundland and Labrador, Fredericton, Montreal, Nova Scotia and Prince Edward Island, Quebec, and Western Newfoundland). The Anglican Military Ordinariate is an autonomous, non-geographical jurisdiction with its own bishop and established structures, and hence is listed separately. Although served by a national Indigenous archbishop, structures for a self-determining Indigenous church within the Anglican Church of Canada are still in development, and therefore not included as a separate category in this survey. The relative absence of Indigenous voices in this study is addressed in the conclusion.

34. At the time of the survey there were forty-two active bishops in the Anglican Church of Canada, so this represents a response rate of 38 percent.

Formation for Transformation

A large majority of respondents (83 percent) prepared for ordained ministry at a residential seminary or theological college, corresponding with the 80 percent of seminary or college administrators who described the primary teaching method of their institution as "residential." Thirty-two percent of respondents were ordained in or since 2010. The remainder were admitted to holy orders in the 2000s (28 percent), the 1990s (20 percent), the 1980s (15 percent), the 1970s (7 percent) or the 1960s (5 percent).

Like the seminary or college administrators who were surveyed, the clergy were asked if they agreed or disagreed with the Joint Working Group's declaration, "Ecumenical formation must be an essential element for candidates for ordained ministry." As with the heads of the seminaries or colleges, the clergy overwhelmingly affirmed this statement, with 90 percent of respondents indicating that they agreed. Among those who attempted to explain why they agreed with the statement, responses such as the following were typical: "My experience in a multi-tradition theological program was so valuable to my formation, my new perspective, my accessing new and innovative ideas and expressions of Christian faith that I would be much poorer and limited in my vision and understanding without it or being restricted to an Anglican-only school."

Two bishops affirmed ecumenical formation as an essential element for ordained ministry based on their own experience of clergy deployment. One observed, "For the past ten years I have been working closely with an ecumenical theological school. I believe that the Anglican students who have been formed in this environment are more able to minister to the wider community." Another said,

> There is an imperative in the gospel for unity—in addition to the practical reality that we need to work together for the sake of the church, especially in small rural communities where trying to sustain multiple denominational congregations is impractical. Without some form of ecumenical formation there is little understanding of our areas of unity or the ways in which we can work together for both practical and theological reasons.

One priest from the Maritimes, whose ministerial formation at a residential seminary did include ecumenical content, related how this can have consequences once one is serving in a ministry context: "Because if this formation does not happen by the time people are being formally trained, it will not happen on the ground in the communities. This is my opinion in dealing with great disappointment with [an] ecumenical clericus."

Similarly, another priest, also serving on the east coast, commented that "formal training encourages future behavior." Another priest reflected ruefully on the consequences of having attended a residential seminary which they indicated offered no ecumenical content—curricular or extracurricular: "Once I started working in parish ministry, and have since worked in five different dioceses, I recognize this gap in my formation. To understand the hermeneutics of my colleagues, I wish my theological education had offered some training in the wider church."

Of the 10 percent of clergy respondents disagreeing with the essential nature of ecumenical ministerial formation, many nevertheless agreed with ecumenism's value, but suggested its place is not in seminaries or theological colleges. Instead, as one priest in southwestern Ontario commented, "The primary focus ought to be on being formed in one's own tradition." Another said, "One must know oneself, as it were, before meaningful dialogue can be undertaken," while still another suggested, "I think this can come through our ministry. I'm not sure we need specific training for this." One respondent concluded that ecumenical formation's time has passed: "There are so many other more urgent areas that need to be addressed that ecumenism hardly seems to be a high priority, at least in my assessment."

Curriculum

Only one third (33 percent) of clergy respondents reported that their ministerial formation included "a course, seminar, or workshop specifically focused on ecumenism." This corresponds closely with the seminary or college survey revealing that only half of those institutions make such an offering, and at only one is it compulsory.

If relatively few clergy participated in an explicit course in ecumenics while at seminary or theological college, a large number reported that several other subjects covered during their ministerial formation did include "an ecumenical dimension or provide perspectives from other Christian traditions." Although these dimensions or perspectives are not defined, a significant number of respondents indicated that ecumenical content of some form was included in their courses on church history (75 percent), pastoral studies (65 percent), biblical studies (56 percent), systematic theology (55 percent), theological ethics (50 percent), and Anglican studies (47 percent). With respect to the denominational diversity of those teaching these courses, 91 percent of clergy respondents replied in the affirmative when asked, "Did any of your instructors belong to another Christian tradition?" This number corresponds almost exactly to the response to the same question offered by the seminaries or colleges.

A number of respondents expanded on their positive experiences of their formal courses of study, including content, perspectives, and/or instructors from Christian traditions other than Anglicanism:

- "The study of church history and the history of Christian thought laid out diverse perspectives and the matters of disagreement between various denominational bodies. Understanding them in their historic setting opens understanding to the 'other' view which was not historically present to critique my denominationally inherited one."
- "In taking courses from different teachers of different denominations, I came to respect their traditions."
- "As a part of the course in modern church history, we had to go to an Orthodox church and interview the priest, and participate as much as possible in one of the services. I chose the Ukrainian Catholic Orthodox Church and had a wonderful experience there."
- "I had several courses in a Roman Catholic college. Discovering the depth of our unity on theological issues was important to preparing me for future dialogue and engagement."
- "Church history classes explained difference[s]. Class and informal discussions helped to overcome them."

The survey further shows that three different ecumenical agreed statements had been read by a majority of respondents. Eighty-six percent indicated they had read *Baptism, Eucharist and Ministry*, the groundbreaking convergence document produced by the WCC in 1982. Seventy percent said they had read *Called to Full Communion: The Waterloo Declaration*, the foundational document bringing the Anglican Church of Canada and the Evangelical Lutheran Church in Canada into a relationship of full communion in 2001. A similar number of respondents (67 percent) indicated that they had read at least one report issued by the Anglican-Roman Catholic International Commission, which have been sporadically issued since 1971. Ten other ecumenical agreed statements listed on the questionnaire had been read by fewer than half of the respondents. What is unclear from the survey is whether respondents had read these documents as a part of their ministerial formation in seminary or theological college, or afterward.

Extracurricular Activities

A very large number of respondents (94 percent) indicated that their cohort of fellow students included at least some non-Anglicans, again reasonably corresponding with the institutional survey's results. When asked if they participated in any extracurricular and/or social activities with these Christians of other traditions, a similarly high number (89 percent) responded positively. Respondents were asked to describe these activities, which included:

- Shared prayer according to different traditions
- Development of ecumenical liturgies
- Participation in the Canadian Theological Students's Conference
- Shared refugee sponsorship
- Meeting and connecting during summer internships
- Week of Prayer for Christian Unity
- Shared retreats
- Participation in the World Day of Prayer
- Mission trips
- Participation in anti-war and anti-poverty demonstrations
- Shared residence accommodations
- Informal gatherings over a meal or drink
- Participation in InterVarsity Christian Fellowship
- Playing music together
- Sports activities
- Informal theology discussion groups
- Visiting one another's churches

Respondents noted that while some of these activities were organized by the institutions at which they were studying, many were the initiative of the students themselves. Though the above list is diverse, three categories of activities were recurrent among many of the respondents: common prayer, informal socializing, and friendships.

Formation for Transformation

The descriptions of common prayer took many forms, including regularly scheduled shared services of worship organized by the school, prayer in the tradition of the ecumenical Taizé community, and informal "prayer circles" organized by the students. A bishop whose priestly training took place in an ecumenical residential context noted the key role of common prayer in his ministerial formation: "I place a high value on the weekly ecumenical worship in my seminary years. Worshipping together deepened our relationships, while helping me understand the different ways of ordering worship."

Informal socializing was frequently described as shared meals, attending parties, sharing coffee and conversation, going to a bar for a drink, and even playing Frisbee. An outworking of such social activities was the development of ecumenical friendships among students of different Christian traditions, which was highlighted by a number of respondents:

- "I had little experience with other denominations prior to my training, and the experience I had had hadn't always been positive. Through befriending future ministers from other backgrounds, I grew in my ability to minister in my own context."
- "Contact, liturgical and social, created friendships and a basis for ongoing relationships."
- "Because of the friendships made, I became more open to and aware of other denominational styles and expressions."

Another respondent also reported how "ongoing friendships" with classmates from other traditions played an important part of their ministerial formation, while another noted that they "had more non-Anglican friends than Anglican" at the ecumenical consortium at which they studied.

Transformational Learning?

Some of the language survey respondents used to describe the impact of their ecumenical experiences during their ministerial formation resembles that encountered in the testimonials offered by former students of the Ecumenical Institute at Bossey, as seen in the previous chapter. There I attempted to demonstrate that one could detect in the accounts of some Bossey alumni evidence of the perspective transformation that is the end result of Mezirow's process of transformational learning. As already outlined, the first stage in this process is a disorienting dilemma prompting an individual to critically reflect on their misconceptions of a particular group, eventually resulting in a permanent change in the way the individual believes and behaves with respect to that group. Can similar evidence be found in the responses of some of this survey's respondents?

Unlike those former Bossey students, none of the Canadian Anglican clergy completing this survey explicitly used the language of transformation to describe the outcome of their ecumenical encounters at seminary or theological college, nor do any name a specific disorienting dilemma that might be understood to initiate the transformational learning process. Nevertheless, one can detect in a number of responses a significant shift in attitude toward non-Anglicans, often prompted by particular kinds of encounters with them. Of the two hundred and six responses, at least sixteen used language strongly suggesting that ecumenical encounters during the course of their ministerial formation substantially challenged their unexamined assumptions about certain non-Anglican Christians such that their perceptions of that ecclesial out-group were positively changed, if not permanently transformed in the sense of Mezirow's theory. For the purposes of further analysis, we will narrow the focus on this smaller group of respondents.

Each of the sixteen responded positively to the question, "Did your ministerial formation in any way change your attitude toward other Christian traditions?" When asked to explain how their attitudes were changed, they each responded as follows:

- "Through personal experience with Christians of other denominations I came to realize the many gifts we all have to offer one another. Through dialogue and in conversation with them, my own prejudices lessened and I became much more open and . . . accepting of other Christian traditions."

- "They helped to see beyond stories or rumors to experience real people and ideas—to identify many ways in which [we] share similar understand[ings] and to be more than simply tolerant of different ideas but accepting and enriched by differences. The way in which the professors respected and encouraged different understandings acted as exemplars for me in my future ministry."

- "I had unexamined biases and stereotyped views, which were changed as I learned more about the other traditions; I had been much more open to other religions than I was to other [Christian] denominations."

- "When I first enrolled in seminary I viewed Roman Catholicism as rather backward and misogynistic. Through my courses at Roman Catholic colleges and interaction with Roman Catholic instructors and students, I came to appreciate their . . . traditions, theology, and spirituality—so much so that I chose a Roman Catholic layperson as my spiritual director."

- "I was enchanted with and challenged by the way my Roman Catholic friends and classmates spoke about Mary. Being in relationship with her made sense to me. I loved hearing students speak about their struggles and how their relationship with Mary gave them comfort. I was challenged by the approach by United Church friends took towards the sacraments and towards worship. I didn't agree with the approach, as liturgy means so much to me, but it was interesting to hear how they described their approach as making room for creativity. I loved my history class at Knox College and the easygoing yet cerebral approach of the professor and class, and learning about Reformed theology in that specifically Calvinist context."

- "I believe it not only gave me an appreciation, but also a lived experience of living beyond our imposed walls/barriers and to work past them—actively working against liberal/conservative, large/small, and other perceived and real differences, to try and find ways to work together."

- "I think I already respected other traditions, but rubbing elbows with them for three years meant that I could talk specifically about what I respected about them."

- "As a person who did not grow up in the church I believe that I learned much from [my seminary] experience as it related to the various traditions I encountered and the need to simply be in relationship with people of other traditions, even when that was as simple as having coffee with a group from diverse backgrounds."

- "I found that I was more accepting after my ecumenical education than before."

- "Just the fact of being around others who thought different than I regarding scripture, theology, ministry, etc., really challenged me and expanded my faith and world in general."
- "I became more open minded, especially toward Protestants. Studying together broke down my Anglo-Catholic prejudices and, to be honest, snobbery."
- "My natural feelings of suspicion about other traditions (because they were different) were removed so that I could listen non-judgmentally and be willing to work together with the other churches."
- "I developed a deeper awareness of and respect for other traditions, particularly Roman Catholic and Orthodox, that I had not encountered much prior to my theological formation."
- "Having grown up in the Anglican tradition, it was enlightening for me to engage with people of different denominations and compare similarities and differences, but more importantly to really get to know people's hearts and passion for serving Jesus Christ. I learned that styles of worship may be different, theology may be somewhat different, but the underlying desire to follow Christ is something that we share."
- "Understanding other traditions through common study and life together gave me a deeper understanding of why I am an Anglican and the deep common threads that hold all Christian traditions together."
- "As an Anglo-Catholic within an historical manifestation of Anglicanism with a profound identity based on ecclesiology formed against the dominant ecclesiological view of the established [Presbyterian] church [in Scotland, where the respondent received his ministerial formation], intolerance of this denomination [the Church of Scotland] was rife. Working with students and ministers from this tradition over a number of years softened my attitudes as I discovered that the stereotypes were unfounded. I would never have received [communion] from a Presbyterian as a teenager. Also, their attitudes toward female ordination helped when my denomination followed."

All but three of the respondents quoted above indicated that the setting for their ministerial formation was residential, more readily affording them opportunities for (in the words of one respondent) "rubbing elbows" with non-Anglicans on a sustained and more intentional basis than someone preparing for ministry through, for example, distance education. (The issue of providing an ecumenical dimension to distance education for ministry will be addressed in a later chapter.) While only six of the sixteen (38 percent) said that they had enrolled in a course, seminar, or workshop specifically focused on ecumenism, all of the respondents indicated that their teachers and fellow students included individuals from Christian traditions other than their own. All but two of the respondents in the subset (88 percent) said that they participated in extracurricular and/or social activities with non-Anglican students during their formation.

According to Mezirow's process of transformational learning, a perspective transformation is achieved when a *permanent* change in an individual's frames of reference has occurred. It is not possible within the limits of this study to establish whether such a permanent change has occurred among any of the respondents. However, the responses above would suggest that within this particular subset of sixteen respondents, the following conclusions can be drawn: (1) a significant change in their perspective and attitudes toward non-Anglicans has occurred; (2) this change was prompted through encounters enabled by their ministerial formation, which was largely residential; and (3) if not permanent, this change in attitude and perspective has endured since they concluded their seminary- or college-based ministerial formation—a time period ranging, depending on the respondent, from six to forty-seven years.

Current Ecumenical Engagement

Has the change in perspective to which this subset of respondents attests carried over not only into their attitudes but also their actions as ministers, and has the ecumenical consciousness they seemed to have developed in seminary or theological college translated into concrete ecumenical involvement in their current ministry contexts?

Before attempting to answer these questions with specific reference to these respondents, however, it will be useful to establish some benchmarks by which to evaluate their replies. The questionnaire asked if the respondents's current ministry includes "any collaboration or engagement with churches and/or individuals from other Christian traditions," and if so what form that collaboration or engagement takes.

One set of benchmarks can be found in the three works on ecumenical engagement reviewed and summarized in chapter 3: *Growing Together*

Surveying Canadian Anglican Ecumenical Formation

in *Unity and Mission*, *A Handbook of Spiritual Ecumenism*, and *Christian Unity: How You Can Make a Difference*. Combined these books make no fewer than seventy-three recommendations (some of which overlap) on how the high degree of unity of faith already achieved between divided churches can be given concrete expression, especially at the level of a local congregation. These suggestions fall into four broad categories: (1) visible expressions of our shared faith, (2) joint study of our shared faith, (3) co-operation in ministry, and (4) shared witness in the world. As observed in chapter 2, these recommendations place a notable emphasis on activities related to our common baptism, common prayer, and the joint study of our common scriptures. Together these suggestions represent a comprehensive list of practical activities which are, in part, among the visible desired outcomes of an effective ecumenical ministerial formation.

Observations and Analysis

Having established some benchmarks for what ecumenical engagement in a congregational context can look like, we can compare them with the responses of the subset of sixteen survey respondents, three-quarters of whom identified their primary context for ministry as congregational. Of the sixteen clergy in this subset twelve are priests, three bishops, and one a deacon. Thirteen of the respondents (81 percent) indicated that their current ministry includes collaboration or engagement with churches or individuals from other Christian traditions. When asked to specify the nature of this collaboration or engagement, these were among the replies:

- "I am treasurer of [an Anglican theological college in an ecumenical consortium], and will soon be working more frequently with the Presbyterian and United Church colleges."
- "I co-founded a children's ministry conference that attracts a variety of Christians. We added some Baptists to the planning team for good measure."
- "Ecumenical services during Wednesday in Lent at 12 noon followed by soup luncheon. Ecumenical service on Good Friday and on the first Sunday in Advent. The area ministerial meets quarterly for a breakfast meeting. Work with the Salvation Army to provide toys for needy children at Christmas. All the area churches provide volunteers

to help with the Salvation Army Kettle Campaign. Various church[es] participate in the Cenotaph Ceremony on Remembrance Day."

- "I work closely with representatives of many denominations and other faith groups on the Interfaith Committee [on] Military Chaplaincy [of the Canadian Council of Churches]. I also provide pastoral care and support to all military chaplains, though my primary responsibility is care of Anglican chaplains."
- "Church choir."
- "Working with other downtown church leaders in areas of social justice."
- "This collaboration is in its early days. My youth group has participated in joint events with youth groups from neighboring Anglican parishes and other Christian denominations. I have been meeting with the new pastors at the local Lutheran church to find ways we can work together. We are beginning with a joint potluck dinner this Sunday. I am also planning to host a KAIROS [an ecumenical peace and justice coalition] 'Reconciliation in the Watershed' workshop in the spring, which I hope will form part of an ecumenical Creation Cares series. (A neighboring United Church is also hosting a Water Walk.)"
- "Working with the local United Church in our local food justice initiatives, supporting each other's events and activities and participating in community events (like the local Remembrance Day service) together. We also do a combined Good Friday walk."
- "Organizing meetings with ecumenical community chaplains; inviting speakers from different faiths to share their faith at The Well drop-in where I work; providing spiritual direction to people from different denominations; providing retreats to people from different faiths."
- "Refugee sponsorship, annual Good Friday walk"
- "Shared cemetery services; ecumenical breakfasts; food cupboard we run together; youth and seniors ride and festival events; refugee sponsors; bazaar coordination; community town hall for faith leaders including interfaith collaboration"
- "Student suppers . . . United Church, Presbyterian, Unitarians; Refugee support [with] Syrian Orthodox Church . . . United Church shared ministry; Week of Prayer for Christian Unity; World Day of Prayer;

Messy Church with United Church . . . university ecumenical chaplaincy . . . ecumenical services."

- "Talking about parenting in the context of faith or no faith"
- "Anglican/Lutheran ventures, as well as many ecumenical endeavors between Anglicans, United Church and Catholics in ministerial groups across the diocese."

These responses offer examples of ecumenical worship, shared community outreach and social justice work, interdenominational partnership in refugee sponsorships and interfaith engagement, joint youth group events and a couple of other kinds of collaboration in Christian formation.

A variety of forms of ecumenical worship are mentioned by these respondents. Three specifically name shared Good Friday commemorations, which is a recommendation found in GTUM. Elsewhere in the survey clergy are specifically asked if they or their congregation in some way observe the Week of Prayer for Christian Unity, and thirteen (81 percent) indicated that they did. Only two respondents (13 percent) said they participated in a "pulpit exchange" with a cleric of another denomination. Another typical form of engagement with clergy of other churches is the so-called local "ministerial," a regular coming together of pastors from different denominations serving in a common area. GTUM, Kasper, and Ryan each recommend such a gathering in some form. In the open-ended question only one respondent above specifically mentioned participation in an "area ministerial," and in a separate close-ended question only three of the sixteen respondents in this subset (19 percent) indicated they participate in one.

When compared to the list of more than seventy possible examples of on-the-ground local ecumenical collaboration outlined, the activities named by these respondents but scratch the surface. None relate to baptism or the study of the scriptures—two areas of possible ecumenical collaboration especially highlighted by GTUM, Kasper, and Ryan.

Also largely absent from these responses is any clearly articulated suggestion that these clergy take the kind of all-encompassing approach to ecumenical engagement envisioned by most of the advocates of ecumenical ministerial formation we have encountered, and encapsulated in the Lund Principle's exhortation that the divided churches do everything they possibly can together. Thomas Ryan points out that this "is not a question of just occasionally joining hands in a joint project, entered into maybe once a year."[35] The responses above suggest, however, that the extent of ecumenical activity in most of these pastors's congregations is sporadic rather than sustained, annual rather than frequent, piecemeal rather than comprehensive, and reflects but a fraction of the possibilities for collaboration with other local churches that have been spelled out in resources like GTUM and the works of Kasper and Ryan. Even though 88 percent of respondents in the overall sample of two hundred and six clergy said they agreed with the statement, "Churches of different traditions should 'act together in all matters except those in which deep differences of conviction compel them to act separately," only one respondent came close to actually expressing this vision of an ecumenical consciousness pervading a priest's approach to congregational ministry when she wrote: "I have been meeting with the new pastors at the local Lutheran church to find ways we can work together."

What conclusions can be drawn from these responses? These sixteen respondents were set apart from the overall group of two hundred and six because they each employed language strongly suggesting that ecumenical encounters during the course of their ministerial formation significantly challenged their unexamined assumptions about certain non-Anglican Christians such that their perceptions of that ecclesial out-group were positively changed. Transformative learning theory, as articulated by Mezirow, assumes that these positively changed perceptions are both permanent and are integrated into the life of the one who is transformed. Can this be said to be the case with these respondents?

Of the sixteen who expressed a substantive change in attitude toward non-Anglicans during the course of their ministerial formation, fourteen (88 percent) reported that their ministries currently include collaboration or engagement of some kind with churches and/or individuals of other Christian traditions. (The nature of that collaboration or engagement is described above.) That is slightly higher than the overall sample of two hundred and six respondents, 82 percent of whom indicated the ministry involves some form of ecumenical encounter. Eighty-eight percent of the subset's respondents attended a residential-style seminar or theological college, with students and faculty from other Christian traditions, affording them curricular and extracurricular opportunities for the kind of ecumenical elbow rubbing described by one priest surveyed. Thirty-eight percent of the subset's respondents indicated that their ministerial formation included a core course in ecumenism. In each of these last two

---

35. Ryan, *Christian Unity*, 46.

categories—attendance at a residential institution and a dedicated course in ecumenism—the subgroup of sixteen scored slightly higher than the overall sample of two hundred and six respondents.

The Limits of the Data Collected

It is admittedly difficult to draw too many definitive conclusions from the data the survey of clergy has generated. For example, can a direct correlation be drawn between the model, setting, and content of one's ministerial formation and their subsequent ecumenical consciousness and engagement? One may not be able to draw such a definitive line between the two. Yet the evidence does suggest that the chances of a Canadian Anglican priest having become more aware and appreciative of other Christian churches and their adherents—and of having that enhanced awareness and appreciation translate into concrete ecumenical engagement in their ordained ministries—increase when their ministerial formation has been primarily residential, has involved non-Anglican students and teachers, has included some ecumenical content in the curriculum, and other liturgical and social activities including non-Anglicans are a part of the overall educational experience. However, a conclusive one-to-one correspondence cannot be made with the data at hand.

In retrospect, different, additional, or more specific survey questions could have been posed that might have helped draw out more definitive data. For example, in addition to being asked, "Did your ministerial formation in any way change your attitudes toward other Christian traditions?" respondents might have also been invited to share some of their particular (negative) attitudes toward non-Anglican Christians *before* they began their ministerial formation, to help better understand how those attitudes had changed. In that same vein, they might have been invited to describe a specific moment, encounter, or experience (akin to Mezirow's "disorienting dilemma") that would have further aided in articulating and unpacking the nature and catalyst of their changed attitude toward other denominations. I will say more in the concluding chapter about how transformative learning theory and ecumenical ministerial formation could enter into a still more interesting and profound conversation than this research has succeeded in engaging.

The survey of Anglican centers of ministerial formation could have also dug deeper. For instance, again in retrospect, another way of approaching the question of ecumenical content in curriculum could have been to simply ask if their institution insists on candidates for ministry completing a core course in ecumenism. (Instead the questionnaire asks the following: "Please list the courses, seminars, workshops, etc., in ecumenism offered by your institution, indicating which (if any) are compulsory for students preparing for ordination, and providing a brief description of each.") Regardless of the answer to the closed-ended question, respondents could have been invited to explain why they do or do not offer a required course in ecumenism. If they do not, is it for economic reasons, overloaded curricula, limited teaching capacity, or theological factors? Some of the possible reasons can still be drawn out from responses to the open-ended questions, but a more direct line of inquiry on the precise reasons why all but one of the responding institutions do not offer any kind of core course in ecumenics would have likely produced useful data.

In addition to these questionnaires, my original research design also included conducting follow-up interviews with selected survey respondents who had indicated a willingness to further participate in this way. Several from both samples did, and provided the necessary contact information. However, a major and highly disruptive shift in my ministry context midway through this research project presented significant obstacles, chiefly in terms of the time I would have at my disposal to first properly conduct and then adequately analyze these interviews. It is likely that illuminating data could have been elicited from a series of interviews with, for example, the subset of sixteen respondents who used language indicating a substantive change in their orientation toward non-Anglicans during the course of their ministerial formation.

In spite of these undoubted limitations, there is still something worthwhile to be harvested from the data resulting from both of these surveys. What they broadly suggest is that ecumenical formation has ceased to be an explicit priority, particularly in terms of curriculum, for the Anglican Church of Canada's principal institutions of theological education. There also appears to be a disconnect between their stated conviction that "ecumenical formation must be an essential element for candidates for ordained ministry" and the degree to which that is actually expressed in the lived experience of their institutions. The data suggests that this naturally influences the lived experience of the future clergy being formed at these institutions. While a large majority of them do have some form of ecumenical engagement in their subsequent ministries, these in general tend to be largely occasional and, one might say, perfunctory, tending to be liturgical and social outreach in nature, less often engaging in shared catechesis and other activities of a more overtly theological bent that might more clearly point to a shared inheritance of faith. Further, a very small number of respondents (8 percent, according to this study) employ language that suggests their attitudes toward non-Anglican Christians were substantially changed during the course of their ministerial formation.

This would all suggest that there is still work to do with respect to the ecumenical formation of those preparing to serve as ordained congregational leaders in the Anglican Church of Canada. Long-standing recommendations for a mandatory core course in ecumenism have not been taken up by the vast majority of seminaries and theological colleges, further suggesting that circumstances call for something different to be proposed if some form of ecumenics has any hope of being taught to postulants for ordination. I will propose such a different approach to the teaching of ecumenics in the following chapter.

5

A Proposed Revised Practice

THE GOAL OF THIS research is to help shape future models of ministerial formation so that all of the baptized of the Anglican Church of Canada can more fully live into the denomination's stated collective commitment to "walk the way of ecumenism."[1] Having explored the current landscape of ecumenical formation in the majority of the institutions at which Canadian Anglican postulants for ordination are receiving their primary formation—and having reviewed the ecumenical experiences of a sample of those institutions's graduates—we can turn to the final movement of practical theology's hermeneutical spiral: the pragmatic task. This, Osmer reminds us, consists of "forming and enacting strategies of action that influence events in ways that are desirable."[2] We therefore take as desirable an ecumenical formation for prospective Canadian Anglican clergy that is widely available, locally applicable, and results in pastors who are ecumenically literate and engaged.

My suggestion for a revised practice for ecumenical ministerial formation in the Anglican Church of Canada will draw from and expand upon a relatively brief proposal developed by American ecumenist Mitzi J. Budde and outlined in an article she published in 2010 as one of several contributors to a wide-ranging anthology on theological education in the twenty-first century.[3] An earlier treatment of this proposal appears in the dissertation for her doctor of ministry degree, which she earned from

1. General Synod, "Towards a Renewed Ecumenical Strategy."
2. Osmer, *Practical Theology*, 176.
3. Budde, "Vocation for Unity," 98–108.

A Proposed Revised Practice

Wesley Theological Seminary in 2004. For that research, Budde conducted an ethnographic study of four American seminaries representing different Christian traditions, comparing their approaches to ecumenical formation, and then proposing a framework for an intentional and potentially transformative ecumenical component for denominationally based theological education. Since 1991 she has been teaching ecumenism at Virginia Theological Seminary. Budde's own scholarly journey reflects her deep commitment to ecumenical formation. A deacon of the Evangelical Lutheran Church in America (ELCA), she completed her doctorate in ministry at the Methodist partner in an ecumenical theological consortium, and is a faculty member at a seminary of the Episcopal Church. She is a former president of the North American Academy of Ecumenists and is a longstanding member of the Lutheran-Episcopal Coordinating Committee, the body which oversees the implementation of the full communion agreement between the ELCA and the Episcopal Church.

After summarizing Budde's proposal, I will suggest how it might be adapted to a Canadian Anglican context, taking into account the findings revealed in the previous chapter and the insights of transformative learning theory. I will also consider the added dimension to this question created by the recent proliferation of theological education offered online, and the challenges that this new delivery method presents for the kind of transformative ecumenical formation that is being considered here.

Budde's 'Proposal for the Future'

Like many others encountered in this study, Budde is persuaded that incorporating an "intentional ecumenical component" into the curriculum, formation process, and community life of institutions dedicated to ministerial formation is a matter of urgency.[4] In part this is because a failure to raise up the next generation of committed ecumenists risks an irredeemable loss of ecumenical memory that, through ignorance of past breakthroughs and existing consensus, puts in jeopardy present and future efforts to reveal the church's visible unity. Rather than becoming agents of reconciliation, they risk perpetuating false narratives and harmful misrepresentations, simply out of ignorance. There is also a pressing need for ecumenically formed Christian leaders, she argues, because we inhabit a society characterized by discord, disagreement, and division—particularly among different faith

4. Budde, "Vocation for Unity," 90.

groups: "In a post-September 11, 2001, world, Christians have a new urgency to find unity within Christianity, in order to speak more clearly and to witness more intelligibly in interreligious dialogue."[5]

As implied by her assessment of the current situation and by offering a proposal to address it, Budde believes the overall state of ecumenical formation in mainline American seminaries falls short of what is necessary to equip priests and pastors to be the kind of agents of reconciliation she believes the churches and the wider world today require. Speaking out of her own experience as a teacher of ecumenics in a single-denomination seminary, she observes that, "When I teach students, usually I find them well educated about these theological divisions [between denominations], but *not* about the decades of ecumenical dialogue that have addressed and, in many cases, bridged these divisions. We re-inculcate the divisions of the church into every successive generation."[6] To inculcate an attitude of unity rather than a spirit of division among prospective clergy, Budde offers in a "Proposal for the Future" a method consisting of three interconnected movements which, following Roman Catholic educator Jane Regan's analysis of adult catechesis, she labels "inform," "form," and "transform."[7] We will briefly look at each in turn.

'Inform'

The "inform" stage of the model is arguably the most didactic, with Budde herself describing it as "teaching the content of ecumenism."[8] It primarily concerns a seminary's curriculum, which she argues must include "at least a basic understanding of other churches's theology, polity, liturgical practices, homiletics, forms of spirituality, and cultures, in a way that engages the other traditions with respect."[9] That respectful engagement is what she says differentiates ecumenical theology from "comparative dogmatics," because the former requires the student to study the theological constructs of the other church "in order to understand it on its own terms before making theological value judgements out of one's own tradition."[10]

5. Budde, "Vocation for Unity," 97.
6. Budde, "Vocation for Unity," 98. Emphasis in original.
7. Budde, "Vocation for Unity," 98–99. See also Regan, *Toward an Adult Church*, 15.
8. Budde, "Vocation for Unity," 99.
9. Budde, "Vocation for Unity," 99.
10. Budde, "Vocation for Unity," 99.

A Proposed Revised Practice

Budde suggests one of the best resources for seminaries to use in such a process of respectful engagement is ecumenical agreed statements, for a number of reasons. First, by studying their own church's bilateral or multilateral agreements with other churches, seminarians can enrich their understanding of their own tradition. It is often through dialogue with another church that a denomination acquires a particular clarity about its own beliefs, traditions, and practices. Further, since ecumenical documents represent a specialized genre of theological literature in their own right, learning to read and assess them constitutes an important skill. Finally, Budde argues, once they are ordained and engaged in a ministry context, these new pastors or priests will have "the opportunity and the responsibility" to bring the ecumenical agreements of their churches into the life and practice of the congregations they will serve.[11]

She also contends that clergy require sufficient understanding of other ecclesial traditions so that they can adequately interpret and respond to congregants who react to a given situation out of a different tradition: "For example, a convert to a tradition that understands its priest or minister as a prophetic leader who stands apart from the congregation might come to a vestry position[12] with an unexamined assumption that the clergyperson is hired staff and a differing expectation about the priest's level of accountability to the governing board of the parish."[13] As I will observe later in this chapter, denominations's differing expectations with respect to other matters, such as sacramental practice, can also become points of friction, further highlighting the value of having ecumenically literate clergy who are prepared to engage constructively when these differences surface.

'Form'

This second movement of Budde's proposal, "form," focusses on a seminarian's extracurricular ecumenical experience, although she prefers describing this as an institution's "implicit curriculum," defined as "the cultural and socializing approaches of the community of learning."[14] In the case of

---

11. Budde, "Vocation for Unity," 100.

12. In this context "vestry" refers to an official body of lay leaders who oversee the temporal (and in some cases also spiritual) affairs of a parish. The term is most frequently used this way in the Anglican tradition.

13. Budde, "Vocation for Unity," 99–100.

14. Budde, "Vocation for Unity," 101.

a seminary these include worship, field education, retreats, and spiritual direction. Such encounters outside the classroom, Budde argues, are necessary complements to the curriculum-based aspects of the first movement of her proposal: "To form seminarians ecumenically means to move beyond the intellectual learnings of the 'inform' stage to a level of experiential education characterized by relationship and encounter."[15]

Key for Budde among these relational ecumenical encounters is common prayer, which she says must extend beyond seminarians simply attending the liturgies of other churches as passive observers: "Seminaries whose chapel practices include liturgies from other denominational traditions and ecumenical worship experiences are providing an experiential component. Prayer for unity creates a hunger for unity."[16] While she does not specifically mention social gatherings or the development of ecumenical friendships among these possible relational encounters, Budde does name "informal groups" and, more generally, "informal experiences" as forms of implicit curriculum.[17]

'Transform'

"Transform" is the third and final stage of the proposal, and is actually the intended result of the first two movements. Budde describes this step in a seminarian's ecumenical learning as nothing less than "conversion," whereby these formal and informal ecumenical experiences of the "inform" and "form" stages combine, "connecting the subject deeply with students's lives and faith systems."[18]

Budde's use of the language of transformation is not coincidental. She too engages with Mezirow's theory of transformative learning, describing it as "a process of change and challenge to one's old worldview that may have painful elements."[19] While placing a particular emphasis on the role of educators in developing methodologies capable of fostering transformative learning experiences, she also acknowledges the challenging nature of that task, admitting that "transformation cannot be scripted."[20] Nevertheless, Budde

15. Budde, "Vocation for Unity," 101.
16. Budde, "Vocation for Unity," 101.
17. Budde, "Vocation for Unity," 101.
18. Budde, "Vocation for Unity," 103.
19. Budde, "Vocation for Unity," 103.
20. Budde, "Vocation for Unity," 103.

offers two means by which the conditions for transformative ecumenical learning can been cultivated within a setting of ministerial formation.

The first regards the individuals who are actually offering the formation. Simply put, instructors ought to come from a variety of different Christian traditions, even if the institution in which they are teaching is primarily aligned with one particular denomination. The mere presence of such teachers from other denominations is itself an implicit recognition of the ecclesiality of the church tradition from which they come. If not of a different ecclesial background themselves, seminary instructors who are involved in ecumenical dialogues, or who are otherwise conversant with other Christian traditions, can help "create a community of learning that reflects the whole church," rather than one single expression of it.[21]

In terms of curricular content, Budde goes on to suggest that churches that have negotiated full communion agreements with other churches could use these bilateral accords as a starting point for offering some initial and intentional ecumenical formation to those preparing for ministry. On the surface, doing so would serve the function of preparing ordinands for the possibility of serving in a full communion partner church. At a deeper level, however, engaging with the content of a full communion agreement in detail would generate the potential for delving deep into the churches's respective differences in faith and order that would have required reconciling before such an agreement of mutual recognition could be entered into. Budde believes that such a sustained engagement with these full communion texts by successive cohorts of those training for ministry could have an impact not only on individual clergy, but on the theology, homiletics, liturgics, spirituality, polity, field education, and culture of the church to which they belong.[22]

A lack of any ecumenical content in a seminary or theological college's curriculum speaks volumes, Budde argues. In contrast to institutions which may manifest at least an "implicit curriculum" of ecumenical formation (such as diverse worship, field education, instructors from other traditions, etc.), a school that offers little or nothing with an ecumenical dimension is (consciously or not) providing a "null curriculum," described as (again following Regan) "what the community does not talk about."[23] As Budde elaborates,

---

21. Budde, "Vocation for Unity," 104.
22. Budde, "Vocation for Unity," 104.
23. Budde, "Vocation for Unity," 102.

> If courses on ecumenism are not offered, or are offered only infrequently, that lacuna becomes a form of null curriculum. The lack of the presence—or the acknowledgement—of adherents of other denominational traditions in a seminary community is also a null curriculum element. Choosing not to observe the Week of Prayer for Christian Unity or some other form of ecumenical worship experience in seminary chapel practice is another null curriculum example.[24]

By failing to provide any explicit ecumenical content or presence, an institution conveys an implicit message to its students: the quest for the full visible unity of the church is dated, irrelevant, optional, or possibly even dangerous.

Assessing Budde's Proposal

In a number of ways Budde's "Proposal for the Future" is but a fresh restatement of past hopes and recommendations for ecumenical ministerial formation, several of which have already been encountered in this book. For example, the Roman Catholic Church, both separately and together with the Joint Working Group with the World Council of Churches (which, as observed earlier, has included significant Anglican participation), advocates both a core course in ecumenism for those training for ordination and the inclusion of an ecumenical dimension to the teaching of all other theological disciplines. Budde's stress on the value of ecumenical common prayer reflects another recurring emphasis on the important role that praying for unity—and doing so with Christians of other traditions, sometimes according to their traditions—can have in making that unity visible. As Yves Congar was apparently fond of saying to his students, "We can pass through the door of ecumenism only on our knees." Budde's stated goal of students of ministry undergoing an ecumenical "conversion" echoes Margaret O'Gara's hope for what might result if her own Catholic Church actually applied more fully its own stated expectations for the ecumenical formation of seminarians.

However, the fact that each of these hopes and recommendations—some of them many decades old—remain largely unfulfilled means that there continues to be a need for constructive restatements of the importance of ecumenical ministerial formation and fresh expressions of how

---

24. Budde, "Vocation for Unity," 102.

A Proposed Revised Practice

it might be offered in the current context of the theological education of those preparing for ordained ministry.

Perhaps Budde's most novel contribution to this ongoing effort is her suggestion that a church's full communion agreements form the basis of an "overview course" in ecumenics. Such an offering would "cover the differing theologies, polities, liturgies, and spiritual practices of those partner churches."[25] It would have the practical outcome of both preparing a priest or pastor to potentially serve in a congregation of a full communion partner, while also bringing to the surface a multiplicity of theological questions—such as liturgy, sacraments, orders, governance, authority, and biblical interpretation—that would have emerged, and presumably been to some extent resolved, during the formal dialogues leading to the full communion agreement's ratification.

In the case of Budde's own church, such a course would be wide ranging indeed. The Evangelical Lutheran Church in America has since 1997 negotiated full communion agreements with six denominations representing a relatively wide ecclesial diversity: the Presbyterian Church (USA), the Reformed Church in America, the United Church of Christ, the Episcopal Church, the Moravian Church, and the United Methodist Church. Exploring the different ecclesiologies, polities, liturgies, sacramental theologies, biblical hermeneutics, and theological ethics operative in just those half-dozen denominations would provide no shortage of material for an introductory course in ecumenism. But Budde's other goal in proposing such an agreement-based course is to equip future congregational leaders such that they can "translate ecumenical agreements into a local church's pastoral practice and spiritual life."[26] This is not simply for the sake of assisting in these agreements's reception at the most local level (although that is indeed one goal), but also because of the ecumenical realities these clergy will likely be facing in their congregational contexts:

> Newly ordained ministers will find themselves dealing with ecumenical issues in the parish such as mixed marriages and pastoral issues (i.e. premarital counselling, baptisms, first communion), blended worship opportunities (both community worship events and bilateral worship with neighboring congregations of other denominations), joint education opportunities (such as Vacation Bible

---

25. Budde, "Vocation for Unity," 104.
26. Budde, "Vocation for Unity," 101–2.

School and joint youth groups), and shared service opportunities (like Habitat for Humanity, literacy tutoring, and food pantries).[27]

Such a course could therefore use a full communion agreement as a launching point for a multiplicity of discussions and learning opportunities that are both deeply theological and pastorally practical, all the while demonstrating the inherent value of ecumenical agreed statements when they are studied, received, and applied.

We will revisit Budde's proposal in an attempt to specifically adapt it to a Canadian Anglican context. However, before doing so we will engage with an increasing reality in the realm of ministerial formation: distance education. Any new proposal for ecumenical ministerial formation—particularly one seeking to be grounded in transformative learning theory—must take this relatively new phenomenon in theological education into account. This was already true before the coronavirus pandemic forced practically every theological college and seminary to at least temporarily move their teaching exclusively online; it is even more so in the wake of COVID-19.

The Challenge of Online Learning

Budde's inform-form-transform proposal assumes a classical residential seminary scenario in which students are regularly on campus—possibly even living in community—and frequently participating in classes, chapel, and other extracurricular activities in person. While this continues to be the standard method of ministerial formation in North American mainline churches, that reality is rapidly changing. As a result, many seminaries and theological colleges are attempting to adapt their curricula, delivery methods, and other practices to a context in which an increasing number of students, either by preference or necessity, pursue their ministerial formation at a distance, usually online. We will briefly survey this rapidly changing landscape and consider some of its implications for the kind of ecumenical formation that is being proposed.

Two decades ago not a single institution accredited by the Association of Theological Schools (ATS) offered any courses online. By 2017 nearly two-thirds of ATS's two hundred and seventy-three member schools had at least some online course offerings.[28] Almost all of those institutions provide

---

27. Budde, "Vocation for Unity," 102.
28. Tanner, "Online Learning," 1.

A Proposed Revised Practice

"comprehensive distance education," defined by ATS as "a mode of education in which students and instructors are not in the same location," noting that the most common form of distance education is "online delivery." To qualify for this formal designation, an institution must demonstrate that it "has the resources and capacity to offer a variety of distance education courses," and is able to offer at least six such courses.[29] Five of the seminaries or theological colleges surveyed for my study have earned this particular ATS accreditation: Atlantic School of Theology, Saint Paul University, Trinity College, Vancouver School of Theology, and Wycliffe College.[30]

The kinds of courses on offer online have also changed rapidly, moving from periodic electives to entire degree programs. The first completely online master of divinity (MDiv) program offered by an ATS-accredited school was inaugurated in 2013. By 2017 one could earn an MDiv, presumably without ever setting foot in a seminary or theological college, through no fewer than two-dozen ATS-accredited institutions.[31] An increasing number of students of ministry are indeed doing so. In a ten-year period from 2007 to 2017 the number of students taking at least one online course at an ATS-accredited institution nearly tripled from eight thousand to twenty-three thousand.[32] This trend in theological education—described by some as a "digital seismic shift"[33]—seems likely to continue, and is not unique to the field of ministerial formation. A recent survey of Canadian universities commissioned by the federal government, for example, revealed that 93 percent of respondents offer some form of online learning.[34]

As more and more theological institutions offer more and more online content, attempts to evaluate the effectiveness of internet-delivered ministerial formation, as compared to teaching offered onsite, are ongoing. In 2016 ATS conducted a survey of member schools offering comprehensive distance education. Among other things the study invited respondents to compare the "educational effectiveness" of its newer online courses compared to its traditional onsite offerings, with definition of this term seemingly left to the respondents to determine according to their own criteria. Among those who did respond, 71 percent indicated that the educational

---

29. Association of Theological Schools, "Petition."
30. Association of Theological Schools "Accredited Schools."
31. Tanner, "Online Learning," 1–2.
32. Tanner, "Online Learning," 2.
33. Reissner, "Examination of Formation," 100.
34. Bates, "National Survey."

effectiveness of their online versus onsite programs was "similar" to that of comparable courses offered onsite.[35]

The same study nevertheless flagged some of the emerging challenges that these institutions were observing as they rolled out their distance education programs. Especially germane to this discussion is that just over one-third of the survey's respondents cited "building relationships" as one of the chief challenges of online education.[36] This mirrors other studies concluding that while there is often no significant difference between distance and onsite programs in terms of achieving course outcomes, "when the face-to-face personal dimension is removed in an online course, concern remains whether the spiritual formation of students can be promoted."[37] This same preoccupation is reflected in ATS's recent study on online formation: "More than other forms of education, *theological* education must attend to the multifaceted development of the person. In addition to intellectual and academic formation and development of skills of ministry, theological students must be formed as persons of integrity and spiritually formed to lead communities of faith and serve in other contexts."[38] Can such formation be effectively offered online? More to the point of this discussion, can the kind of transformative ecumenical formation envisioned by Budde and O'Gara, and experienced by theological students in residential contexts such as Bossey, be engendered in a learning environment in which students rarely—or ever—encounter each other in a classroom, chapel, or any other physical setting?

At least one prominent ecumenist suggests that it cannot. Much of Thomas Ryan's commitment to the full visible unity of the church was born out of his own firsthand experiences of encountering, living among, and worshipping with Christians of other traditions. A champion of ecumenism for more than thirty years, Ryan is persuaded not only of the urgent need to raise up a new generation of ecumenists "who have a fire in their hearts," but also that the best way to kindle that flame is through face-to-face encounters: "Our current educational trends of distance and online learning can lead away from intentional community as a preparation for ministry and pastoral leadership. There is no substitute for up-close interpersonal

---

35. Tanner, "Online Learning," 3.
36. Tanner, "Online Learning," 4.
37. Naidoo, "Ministerial Formation," 3.
38. Association of Theological Schools, "Educational Models," 9. Italics in original.

connection."³⁹ A similar apprehension has been articulated by those who have reflected on the impact on students attending the Ecumenical Institute, one expressing the concern that practices such as distance learning and off-campus classrooms "fly in the face of the sort of profoundly experiential transformation available at Bossey," and risks robbing pastors in training of "experiences that teach the sorts of coping skills Bossey graduates have found so useful ministering amidst the diversity and confusion of a North America that will only become more so in the future."⁴⁰

As early as 1993—when the internet was still in a nascent state—the Joint Working Group between the Roman Catholic Church and the World Council of Churches presciently observed that "the possibilities of mass communication can be an asset for communicating the ecumenical spirit," while at the same time cautioning that "the world of the media has its own logic and values," and that "critical caution must therefore be exercised in availing ourselves of the media for the ecumenical task."⁴¹ At the same time there is a growing body of evidence suggesting that the kind of community and connection that Ryan and others deem essential to the development of an ecumenical consciousness and commitment in future clergy can to some extent be inculcated in an online learning environment as much as in a residential setting.

Among these is a notable 2016 study comparing the formational experiences of ten exclusively online students and ten on-campus students following the same courses toward the same degree through an evangelical theological college in New Zealand. The study found that there were "no significant differences across the formational maturity or spiritual growth trajectories across the on-campus and distance student samples."⁴² More than that, the researcher observed that "both distance and on-campus students talked about their study experiences in terms that echo Mezirow's theory of transformative learning, even though transformative learning theory was not introduced at any stage into the interview."⁴³ While the study noted that on-campus students related that the most useful conversations in this respect were with students of other opinions "that took place informally on campus, outside the classroom," their off-campus classmates were also shaped by the

---

39. Ryan, *Christian Unity*, 128, 130.
40. Delloff, "Embracing Estrangement," 22.
41. Joint Working Group, *Seventh Report*, §25.
42. Nichols, "Formational Experiences," 18.
43. Nichols, "Formational Experiences," 26.

diversity of others's views: "For distance students, others's perspectives included not just those they discussed online but also their engagement with course materials that highlighted alternative faith traditions."[44]

The New Zealand study—and it is but one study—challenges the conventional assumption that a theological student's spiritual formation is in some fundamental way tied to their presence on campus. It concludes that theological education in a community context can be transformative in itself, "regardless of the educational model applied."[45] If so, how could the kind of transformative ecumenical formation envisioned be provided at a distance, by means of an online course, for example?

It would necessarily require the participation of students from different Christian denominations. Though the college that was the setting for the New Zealand study stood in the evangelical tradition, there was sufficient theological diversity among the students (particularly with respect to biblical interpretation) that the resulting engagements produced a transformative effect in at least some of the students. For instance, one related that after the course, "I struggle to see stuff the way I used to." Another stated, "I didn't expect [theological study] to change me much, but it's actually transformed me into a completely different person."[46] A South African scholar in theological education, Marilyn Naidoo, has similarly thought about how the diversity present among a group of distance education students can help produce such outcomes: "[I]t is possible to design online learning to leverage differences that exist between students, by intentionally creating diverse working groups within a course."[47] (In an earlier chapter we saw how John Ford attempted to do this with an on-campus cohort of students from different denominations, asking them to develop a consensus report on a particular theological or pastoral issue.) The New Zealand researcher cited above noted how carefully selected course materials can also contribute to helpfully challenging online students's preconceptions. Notwithstanding the research suggesting that theological education delivered online can still have a transformative impact and result in adequate spiritual formation similar to that of an on-campus experience, Naidoo concludes that a hybrid of the two is preferable to an exclusively online delivery—a combination of face-to-face and digital learning opportunities: "This model blends the best

44. Nichols, "Formational Experiences," 24.
45. Nichols, "Formational Experiences," 29.
46. Nichols, "Formational Experiences," 24, 25.
47. Naidoo, "Ministerial Formation," 3.

A Proposed Revised Practice

of traditional on-campus teaching and learning with online or technology-mediated resources, emphasizing depth as well as access."[48]

Online courses are intended to widen access to educational opportunities to those who would otherwise be unable to be physically present on a campus. However, assumptions about such widespread access cannot always be made, and this will be touched on in the conclusion.

The Limitations of the Current Context

This fourth movement of practical theology's hermeneutical spiral invites the researcher to suggest a revised practice that creates the possibility for "the initial situation to be transformed into ways which are authentic and faithful," based on the findings revealed in the earlier, descriptive and analytical stages of the research.[49] Osmer calls this the "pragmatic task," and pragmatism is indeed a necessary ingredient in considering a revised practice for ecumenical ministerial formation in the Anglican Church of Canada that has any realistic chance of being taken up.

The ideal method for ecumenical ministerial formation remains that which has been expressed a number of different ways throughout this book: (1) a curriculum mandating a core course in ecumenics along with an ecumenical dimension in the teaching of every other theological discipline (Budde's "inform" stage); (2) that curriculum is delivered in a setting that includes instructors, field supervisors, and fellow students from a variety of Christian traditions, as well as regular extracurricular ecumenical opportunities such as common prayer and social activities ("form"); (3) the content and method combine to cultivate an overall environment ripe for transformative learning experiences with the potential to generate in students a lifelong and active commitment to the full visible unity of the church in all its expressions, similarly equipping the people they serve to in turn become agents of reconciliation in their respective communities ("transform").

The seminaries and theological colleges surveyed have in general indicated a lack of capacity or sense of need to provide this holistic vision of ecumenical ministerial formation. As observed in chapter 4, several schools that do not offer an explicit course in ecumenism insist that field is covered implicitly through the content of other courses or the interdenominational makeup of the student body and/or the consortium to which the school

48. Naidoo, "Ministerial Formation," 3.
49. Swinton and Mowat, *Practical Theology*, 97–98.

belongs. Some also argue that their students receive adequate ecumenical exposure—again implicitly—through informal interactions with non-Anglican students and faculty. While this is, indeed, one of the important means by which a seminarian can develop an ecumenical consciousness, those interactions are ideally complemented by curricular moments for critical reflection on some of the questions these encounters might provoke. Failing to combine the two is a lost opportunity.

In that same chapter, Alan Hayes suggested that in the particular context of the Toronto School of Theology, the degree requirements of a given student's home college may leave little room for courses at a college of another tradition. He even noted that the TST's member colleges have a financial disincentive in having their students take courses at other schools in the ecumenical consortium. The continuing trend away from on-campus learning to distance education is another factor to be considered, especially since most of the Anglican institutions being considered here are delivering an increasing amount of their content through online courses.

A further variable is that each of these centers of ministerial formation, though "associated" with the Anglican Church of Canada, is in no way under the juridical authority of the General Synod. They are all separately incorporated, governed by their own structures, and accountable—particularly with respect to curriculum questions—to different constituencies. These can include other colleges or universities to which they are affiliated, accrediting bodies like ATS, and sometimes even local bishops or dioceses. The closest the General Synod has recently come to attempting to influence the curriculum content for candidates for ordination has been the *Competencies* document (see chapter 2), which goes to some effort in pointing out its own lack of binding authority on those engaged in ministerial formation. In any case, its recommendations with respect to ecumenical formation are minimal. All of this suggests that from both a cultural and systemic perspective, neither persuading nor mandating these seminaries or theological colleges to implement the kind of ecumenical formation envisioned here seems like a realistic or pragmatic approach.

The vision of a holistic, potentially transformative approach to ecumenical ministerial formation expressed above remains the ideal and goal. But how can a form of it be adapted to the current context, whose circumstances do not favor its widespread implementation? To begin an answer, we will return to Budde's proposal.

A Proposed Revised Practice

Education for Implementing Ecumenical Agreements

As noted above, Budde's concrete proposal for a way forward in ecumenical ministerial formation is "an overview course focused on a church's full communion partners" and this constitutes the proposed revised practice of her own doctor of ministry research.[50] In her dissertation she notes that such a course should be a particular priority for her own church because the ELCA is in full communion with six other U.S. based denominations, and these agreements include interchangeability of clergy. As a result, Budde argues, "The ELCA seminaries are now not only responsible for teaching students to serve as effective pastors in the ELCA. In addition, they ought to be considering how to train Lutheran students for potential service in the churches of their full communion partners."[51] With so many full communion partners representing a wide variety of Christian traditions—Episcopal, Methodist, Moravian, United, Presbyterian, and Reformed—Budde acknowledges that "it would be impossible to prepare all [ELCA] students for all the potential full communion exchanges."[52] However, even if these nascent Lutheran pastors are not eventually called to serve in a congregation of one of their denomination's full communion partners, Budde argues that they will still inevitably find themselves dealing with ecumenical issues in their ELCA parish—from interchurch marriages to joint service projects with neighboring congregations—and therefore need the kind of foundational ecumenical formation that an overview course in their church's full communion agreements would provide.

The Lutheran World Federation has also noted the intrinsic link between the ecumenical formation of pastors in training and the developing of an ecumenical consciousness among the people they will eventually serve, and has specifically identified the use of church-to-church agreed statements as a useful tool of ecumenical learning: "An identified missing step is allowing [ecumenical] dialogue statements to be a part of the formation of clergy, and then being appropriated into the lives of congregations."[53]

It is a form of this model that I propose as a revised practice in ecumenical ministerial formation for the Anglican Church of Canada, one adapted to both my denomination's ecclesial context and the current

---

50. Budde, "Vocation for Unity," 104.
51. Budde, "Ecumenical Formation," 155–56.
52. Budde, "Vocation for Unity," 105.
53. Joint Working Group, *Reception*, 19.

realities of theological education. One of its goals would be akin to Budde's: to prepare Canadian Anglican priests for the possibility of serving in a full communion (or more broadly ecumenical) context. This would be a practical course outcome, in part attempting to address the desire expressed by some of the seminary respondents that ecumenical formation be pragmatic in its application. However, as I will attempt to demonstrate, learning about the practical implications of ecumenical agreed statements will inevitably also result in an engagement with significant theological issues. It would also respond to one of the Joint Working Group's appeals to the churches with respect to ecumenical formation, namely that they "ensure that the fruits of ecumenical dialogue and cooperation are well known and accessible."[54]

Budde does not delve deeply into what the specific content of such a course for implementing full communion agreements might be, only suggesting that it "probably ought to include elements of theology, homiletics, liturgics, spirituality, polity, field education, and the culture of the other church."[55] Neither does she propose a one-size-fits-all approach to ecumenical ministerial formation. However, my proposal will seek to be specific enough in terms of content and delivery, in hopes of demonstrating both its value and optimizing the chances of its actual implementation.

Speaking out of her American context, Budde laments that "the denominations that have full communion agreements are not yet preparing their students to serve in the other denominations's parishes."[56] There is little to suggest the situation is much different in the Anglican Church of Canada. Fewer than half of the responding seminaries or theological colleges indicated that the Waterloo Declaration—the foundational document with respect to full communion with the Evangelical Lutheran Church in Canada—was in some way incorporated into course readings. A single responding school indicated that one of their students was completing a field placement in an ELCIC congregation.

Because the Anglican Church of Canada currently has only one nationally negotiated full communion agreement (that with the ELCIC) Budde's proposal for education aimed at implementing full communion agreements will need adapting. An entire course could easily be constructed around the full communion agreement with the ELCIC and its theological and practical implications. However, this would be of arguably limited value to

---

54. Joint Working Group, *Reception*, 65.
55. Budde, "Ecumenical Formation," 156.
56. Budde, "Vocation for Unity," 104.

prospective Anglican clergy preparing to serve in places such as Newfoundland and Labrador, Nunavut, or Prince Edward Island, where no ELCIC congregations exist. It would also needlessly limit the scope of what would likely be an Anglican student's only formal introduction to ecumenism.

Instead I propose a course whose content would center on and seek to help enhance the reception and implementation of as many as four ecumenical agreed statements of which the Anglican Church of Canada is a part, directly or indirectly:

- *Initiation into Christ*—A 1991 study document of the Faith and Witness Commission of the Canadian Council of Churches centered on a 1975 mutual recognition of baptism agreement among the Anglican, Lutheran, Presbyterian, Roman Catholic, and United churches in Canada.
- **Called to Full Communion: The Waterloo Declaration**—The 2001 document outlining the full communion agreement between the Anglican Church of Canada and the Evangelical Lutheran Church in Canada;
- *Ecumenical Shared Ministries Handbook*—Produced in 2011 (and revised in 2019) by a joint task force of the Anglican Church of Canada, the Evangelical Lutheran Church in Canada, the United Church of Canada, and the Presbyterian Church in Canada;
- *Growing Together in Unity and Mission*—The 2007 document issued by the International Anglican-Roman Catholic Commission on Unity and Mission.

We will look briefly at each document in turn, considering why each might be a useful resource for those preparing for congregational ministry, and also as a gateway to a discussion about the deeper theological issues to which each of them points.

Initiation into Christ

The first document I propose for inclusion in this course is the oldest and probably least known of the four. My suggestion for its use as a resource is, in part, to help provide the text with the wider audience it merits, and also because it is entirely the work of Canadian theologians representing a wide variety of Christians traditions. Entitled *Initiation into Christ: Common Teaching and Ecumenical Reflections on Preparation for Baptism*, the document was produced in 1991 by the Commission on Faith and Witness, the multilateral theological roundtable of the Canadian Council of Churches (CCC).

The catalyst for the document was the ecumenical consensus emerging around baptism, first expressed by the first World Conference on Faith and Order in 1927 ("We believe that baptism administered with water in the name of the Father, the Son, and the Holy Spirit, for the remission of sins, we are baptized by one Spirit into one body."[57]), and affirmed in 1964 by the Second Vatican Council ("[A]ll who have been justified by faith in baptism are members of Christ's body, and have a right to be called Christian, and so are correctly accepted as brothers [and sisters] by the children of the Catholic Church."[58]). In 1982, Faith and Order catalogued the churches's "remarkable degree of agreement" on baptism (as well as on the eucharist and ministry) in the groundbreaking convergence text, *Baptism, Eucharist and Ministry*.[59]

This growth in a common understanding of baptism across traditions led to a number of mutual recognition agreements in different parts of the world, including in Canada in 1975, when the Presbyterian, Lutheran, United, Roman Catholic, and Anglican ("PLURA") churches agreed that "baptisms conferred with flowing water accompanied by the Trinitarian formula be accepted as valid."[60] This meant that any lingering doubts about the fullness or efficacy of this rite of Christian initiation of any of the churches involved were laid to rest, and individuals moving from one church to another for whatever reason would not be baptized again (or "conditionally" baptized) by the receiving church.

Given the agreement achieved internationally and domestically on the meaning and practice of baptism, the CCC's Faith and Witness Commission thought "it might be possible to develop a common catechesis on baptism."[61] Representatives from thirteen different denominations participated in the text's creation, including some from traditions that only practice adult baptism or eschew baptism altogether. The result was a thirty-page document that "presents common elements identified in the commission's reflection on scripture, theology, and experience which are

57. Faith and Order Secretariat, *Reports*, 15.
58. *Unitatis Redintegratio*, §3.
59. World Council of Churches, *Baptism, Eucharist and Ministry*, vi.
60. Commission on Faith and Witness, *Initiation into Christ*, 3.
61. Commission on Faith and Witness, *Initiation into Christ*, 3.

A Proposed Revised Practice

pertinent in the preparation of individuals for initiation into the body of Christ."[62] Despite that somewhat scholarly self-description, the document is relatively accessible and structured in such a way as to be used in a congregational setting, using scripture, reflections, and discussion questions to engage participants in a reflection on the meaning of baptism. Indeed, the first among the various suggested uses for the text is "with those people considering baptism for themselves or for their children, or those making a personal profession of faith."[63]

The preparation of an ecumenical catechesis on baptism was a commendably audacious initiative on the part of the Faith and Witness Commission. Indeed, it was an even more daring enterprise than the formulation of a common certificate of baptism for the five Canadian churches that were party to the 1975 mutual recognition agreement. The churches were not able to agree on a common baptismal certificate. (As the ecumenical officer of one of the participating churches wryly observed on the fortieth anniversary of the agreement, "I think it's absolutely hilarious that the churches could agree on something as theologically important as baptism, and they couldn't agree on the piece of paper that said it was done the right way."[64])

All five of those denominations were around the table that developed *Initiation into Christ*, but it is unclear to what degree the document was used or made available by the churches that actually created it. Such is frequently the fate of ecumenical agreed statements. Significant human and financial resources are dedicated to an ecumenical project (*Initiation into Christ* was five years in the making), but often little consideration is given to reception—developing a means or strategy to help the text find purchase with their intended audiences so that they can be taken up into the life and practice of the faithful. Therefore, one objective of proposing the use of *Initiation into Christ* is to attempt to enhance its reception, at least within the Anglican Church of Canada, albeit nearly thirty years after its release.

Another goal of using this particular text is to highlight to a generation of Anglican clergy one of the most substantial achievements of theological ecumenism in Canada. As has been noted more than once, our ecumenical memory is fading. More than half of this research's clergy survey respondents were ordained after the year 2000. Significant ecumenical accords brokered before some of these clergy were even born, like the 1975 mutual

---

62. Commission on Faith and Witness, *Initiation into Christ*, 4.
63. Commission on Faith and Witness, *Initiation into Christ*, 4.
64. Gardner, "Canadian Churches."

recognition of baptism agreement, need to be explicitly brought their attention, otherwise these hard-won achievements risk fading away, along with their implications.

One of those implications centers on what another, more recent Faith and Order convergence text calls "the dynamic and profound relation between baptism and the eucharist."[65] More specifically, if a church fully recognizes another's baptism, what are the larger sacramental and ecclesial implications of such a recognition? The late Methodist ecumenist Geoffrey Wainwright is among those who suggests that if baptism and eucharist's dynamic and profound relationship is taken seriously, then the churches that have recognized others's baptisms must accept and engage with the corollary:

> We may wonder whether baptism can have been *recognizably* performed *without* giving access to Holy Communion. The historic and continuing existence of rival eucharistic communities calls the celebration of baptism into question. If now, in an ecumenical situation, mutual recognition of baptism starts to take place, the possible implication for eucharistic admission across ecclesiastical lines must at least be investigated—and therewith the question of mutual ecclesial recognition gets further opened up and the solution of churchly reconciliation perhaps brought closer.[66]

Because of its ecclesial breadth, *Initiation into Christ* also holds the potential to open doors of dialogue with churches that have not typically been a part of the ecumenical movement, such as those in the evangelical tradition. These churches have been experiencing notable growth in many places, including across Canada, and finding common ground on a shared practice such as baptism could lead to further growth in agreement and thus create pathways for common mission.

So, like the other three documents that will be proposed for this course, *Initiation into Christ* has the ability to function at two levels. It is a practical document, one that participants in the course could actually use or adapt for the purposes of baptismal preparation or other forms of catechesis. Indeed, such collaborative efforts in faith formation are just the kind of thing recommended in other documents such as *Growing Together in Unity and Mission* and in the works of Kasper and Ryan. It is at the same time a thoroughly theological document, that can also lead to deeper discussions about the

---

65. World Council of Churches, *Church*, §42.
66. Wainwright, "One Baptism," 471–72. Emphasis in original.

meaning and practice of rites of Christian initiation, how they are differently understood in various traditions of the church, and what the wider implications of churches's recognizing each other's baptisms might be.

Making *Initiation into Christ* the documentary starting point for this course will highlight that mutual recognition of baptism is itself the sacramental and theological starting point from which flows all other ecumenical practice, including the activities that will be covered in other three texts the course would consider.

Called to Full Communion: The Waterloo Declaration

Twenty years since entering into a relationship of full communion, the Anglican Church of Canada and the Evangelical Lutheran Church in Canada are still learning what it means to live in an ecclesial relationship "in which each maintains its own autonomy while recognizing the catholicity and apostolicity of the other, and believing the other to uphold the essentials of the Christian faith."[67] The Waterloo Declaration (as it is most commonly known, named for the Ontario city that was host to Anglican and Lutheran national convocations that ratified it in 2001) provides an overall framework for the implications of this ultimate expression of ecclesial mutual recognition. Among the practical outworkings of the full communion agreement is that clergy from one denomination may serve interchangeably in the other.

The 2001 Declaration itself was silent on the modalities of such interchangeability of ministries, but in 2003 a short ancillary document entitled "Anglican-Lutheran Guidelines for Clergy Serving in Each Other's Churches" was produced. The guidelines are brief and mostly administrative in content, addressing matters like police background checks, remuneration, pension, benefits, and discipline. A small section entitled "Orientation" states: "The receiving bishop shall appoint a mentor to assist the clergy person in acquiring a working knowledge of the polity and practice of the receiving church, and to be available as a resource during the course of the appointment."[68] It goes onto suggest that such an orientation should include:

- Constitutions or canons of congregation, synod or diocese and national church;
- ELCIC Statement on Sacramental Practices;

67. "Preface," in Leggett, *Companion to the Waterloo Declaration*, 13.
68. General Synod, "Anglican-Lutheran Guidelines."

- Any guidelines presently in effect in the synod or diocese and national church;
- Conduct of worship and pastoral care in that church;
- Introduction to the theological emphases of the receiving church.

No further guidance is offered with respect to the form or content of formation of the priest or pastor being received. The assumption seems to be that the individual cleric would have little or no prior experience of the other church's polity, liturgy, or "theological emphases," and that all of this orientation would occur on an *ad hoc* basis after their appointment to serve in the other denomination.

The need for a more structured and intentional formation about our full communion partner may not have seemed as evident in 2003, when the two churches still lived in relative isolation, as it might today. In 2019 there were no fewer than eighty so-called "Waterloo Ministries" across Canada. These are defined as Anglican and Lutheran communities which in some way share facilities, programs, worship, and/or clergy. Congregations that are served by an ordained person of the other denomination are also classified as Waterloo Ministries, as are "merged/combined communities," sometimes also referred to as "joint Anglican-Lutheran parishes."[69] Five such hybrid congregations existed as of 2019. At least five more congregations in the country have clergy from the other full communion partner serving as their priest or pastor. There is every reason to believe that this trend will continue into the future. Anglican clergy will therefore increasingly need to develop, as Budde puts it, "a bilingual familiarity" with both their own tradition and that of the ELCIC, because even if they do not end up serving in some form of Waterloo Ministry, they ought to nevertheless become conversant with the particular pastoral practices, governance structures, and theological understandings of our full communion partner.[70]

The importance of knowing and understanding the similarities and differences between these two churches is in some ways only becoming evident as full communion enters its third decade, and a generation of clergy with no memory of the Waterloo Declaration's inauguration, or the theological dialogues that made it possible, move into church leadership. In recent years the full communion relationship has been strained by different understandings of the rite of confirmation and presidency of the

69. General Synod, "Waterloo Ministries Directory."
70. Budde, "Ecumenical Formation," 145.

eucharist.[71] Clergy who are more conversant in the Waterloo Declaration—and the theological dialogue and principles that undergird it—may find themselves better equipped to positively navigate these and other emerging ecumenical challenges nationally and locally.

In Called to Common Mission, a similar agreement that brought the U.S. based Episcopal Church and the Evangelical Lutheran Church in America into full communion (also in 2001) each church promised "to encourage its people to study each other's basic documents."[72] The Waterloo Declaration has no such provision. Neither does it (or its accompanying commentary) make any explicit reference to how full communion might factor into the ministerial formation of each church's clergy or any other means of encouraging the agreement's reception. In retrospect this would appear to be a significant oversight of the Declaration's framers, one that two decades on has yet to be clearly addressed. This provides still more reasons to include the Waterloo Declaration and its related guidelines as part of an overview course in ecumenism for Canadian Anglican clergy.

In terms of specific course content, reading material would not need to include much more than the Waterloo Declaration itself (perhaps in the form of *A Companion to the Waterloo Declaration*, which also includes commentary and elucidating essays); subsequently issued guidelines concerning clergy mobility, worship practices, and joint parishes; and texts concerning the contemporary confirmation and eucharistic controversies, all of which are available online. Those primary texts would both reveal in concrete ways the practical implications of full communion at a local level, but also open the door to potentially deeper engagement with issues of ecclesiology, liturgy, and sacramental theology that lie at their root of this ecumenical agreed statement.

Ecumenical Shared Ministries Handbook

The joint Anglican-Lutheran parishes that began emerging in the wake of the Waterloo Declaration were in fact predated by a similar phenomenon that became known as ecumenical shared ministries (ESMs). These can take many different forms, but broadly defined they are communities of different Christian traditions that "live in covenanted partnerships, sharing

---

71. See Myers, "Gift Yet to Be Received," 458–70; and Jennings and Myers, "Background and Reflections."

72. Episcopal Church "Agreement of Full Communion," §4.

worship and ministry, while remaining in good standing with the two or more denominations they formally represent."[73]

In North America the first such ecumenical experiments can be traced to eighteenth-century Pennsylvania, where German and Swedish immigrants formed hybrid Lutheran-Reformed congregations. In Canada they first emerged in the early 1900s in the form of "Local Union Churches." Inspired by merger talks among Canadian Methodists, Presbyterians, and Congregationalists, these "local groups of people founded new congregations unattached to any existing denomination."[74] By the time the United Church of Canada formally came into being in 1925, there were an estimated one hundred Local Union Churches across the country, and collectively they formed a fourth stream of churches founding the new denomination.

It was another prospective denominational merger that prompted the next wave of ecumenical shared ministries in Canada. By the 1960s organic union talks between the Anglican Church of Canada and the United Church of Canada were underway. Inspired in somewhat the same manner as the Local Union Churches several decades earlier, Anglican and United Church congregations in the late 1960s and early 1970s began entering into formal partnerships in anticipation of their denominations's merger. The ground for these ecumenical shared ministries was particularly fertile in southeastern British Columbia, where at the peak of their cooperation the local Anglican diocese and United Church presbyteries gave their blessing to the creation of sixteen shared congregations.[75]

The proposed Anglican-United Church merger was scuttled in 1975, but the shared congregations that were supposed to be a foretaste of that organic union endured, and several still exist to this day. They are among more than one hundred ecumenical shared ministries across Canada currently catalogued by the Prairie Centre for Ecumenism, with Anglicans in some way participating in ninety-two of them.[76] While most of the ESMs involving Anglicans have the ELCIC or United Church as partners, some also include the participation of the Presbyterian Church in Canada or Mennonite Church Canada.

Ecumenical shared ministries have, in one form or another, been a part of the Canadian ecclesial landscape for more than a century now. While

73. Beardsall et al., "Space for the Other," 152.
74. McIntire, "Unity among Many," 7.
75. McCullum, *Radical Compassion*, 114.
76. Prairie Centre for Ecumenism, "Ecumenical Shared Ministries Directory."

A Proposed Revised Practice

some are carryovers from the unconsummated Anglican-United Church union, several others have been established in recent years. On occasion their creation is motivated by non-theological factors like demographic and financial exigency. Sometimes they come into being through the prompting of agreements like the Waterloo Declaration. Whatever the motivating factors, there is every reason to believe that ecumenical shared ministries will continue to be a local ecclesial reality for years to come, and that Anglicans will continue to be significant participants. Therefore, any practical ecumenical ministerial formation offered to prospective Canadian Anglican clergy ought to include some engagement with the concept of ESMs.

The principle document to resource such an engagement is the *Ecumenical Shared Ministries Handbook*, a document produced in 2011 (and revised in 2019) by the Ecumenical Shared Ministries Task Force, a joint body of the Anglican Church of Canada, the Evangelical Lutheran Church in Canada, the Presbyterian Church in Canada, and the United Church of Canada.

The *Handbook* is framed as "an information package to help interested Christians explore the possibilities of ecumenical shared ministry at the congregational level."[77] It stresses that it is not an authoritative document, since every ESM will be unique and ultimately subject to the policies of each of the participating denominations. Nevertheless, the document helpfully highlights several of the pastoral and theological issues that might arise in the formation of an ecumenical shared ministry. For example, how are sacraments administered in an ESM congregation when there is not yet a formal mutual recognition of ministry between the participating denominations? To which ecclesiastical authority is the ordained cleric accountable? How are different worship traditions honored and reconciled? The *Handbook* does not attempt to answer such questions, but rather flags them as the kinds of issues that will need addressing in any negotiation to establish a congregational ecumenical shared ministry. Even more than joint Anglican-Lutheran parishes, ESMs by their very nature can provoke fundamental questions with respect to ecclesiology, ministry and orders, and liturgical and sacramental theology. Indeed, some scholars are attempting to articulate the unique and emerging ecclesiology to which ecumenical shared ministries give expression.[78]

---

77. Ecumenical Shared Ministries Task Force, *Ecumenical Shared Ministries Handbook*.

78. Beardsall et al., *Daring to Share*, 154–70.

At a somewhat more mundane level, another virtue of the *Handbook* as a resource for such a course is that it includes a brief summary of the worship traditions and governance and accountability structures of the four participating churches, as well as a glossary that compares how various terms are used and understood differently in those same ecclesial traditions.

Growing Together in Unity and Mission (GTUM)

A summary of this document of the International Anglican-Roman Catholic Commission on Unity and Mission was provided in chapter 2, so here we will focus more on the reasons why this document merits inclusion in the course I propose.

While the Catholic Church is not (yet) in a relationship of full communion with the Anglican Church of Canada, it is one of my denomination's oldest official dialogue partners. This intimate ecclesial relationship is born in part out of the fact that Anglicanism is the result of a direct rupture between the Church of England and Rome, a history alluded to by Vatican II's acknowledgement of the "special place" occupied by the Anglican Communion among those churches separated from the Catholic Church during the Reformation.[79]

The Anglican-Roman Catholic Dialogue of Canada has been the principle forum for theological encounter between the two churches since 1971, and a separate episcopal roundtable, the Anglican-Roman Catholic Bishops's Dialogue of Canada, was established two years later. Together and separately these dialogues have produced a number of statements on theological convergence as well as pastoral guidelines related to such practical matters as interchurch marriages, eucharistic hospitality, and the transfer of clergy from one communion to the other.

The Roman Catholic Church is also my church's largest ecumenical partner. The 2011 federal census (the most recent government data available for religious affiliation) indicated that nearly 39 percent of Canadians identified as Catholic. Pew Research Center data from 2018 suggests that number is now closer to 29 percent. In either case, Catholicism remains the single largest religious expression in Canada and, unlike Lutheranism, has a physical presence in every part of the country. There are few Anglican congregations in this land that would not have a Catholic parish in relatively close proximity.

---

79. *Unitatis Redintegratio*, §13.

A Proposed Revised Practice

Growing Together in Unity and Mission points its readers toward multiple possible vectors of Anglican-Roman Catholic engagement at every level, especially locally, much of it seemingly untried. Given Catholicism's relative ubiquitousness in Canada (not to mention globally), and "the very impressive degree of agreement in faith that already exists" between the two communions,[80] inviting prospective Anglican clergy to engage with GTUM seems obvious from the standpoint of an ecumenist. Because of the way the document it structured, it would (like the Waterloo Declaration and its associated documents) open doors for discussion about both practical expressions of Anglican-Roman Catholic common mission and the theological factors that have made such unity in mission possible, as well as the areas of continuing theological disagreement. The aforementioned made-in-Canada documents—particularly those regarding interchurch marriage and eucharistic hospitality when Roman Catholics are involved—would provide particularly helpful resources on two pastoral situations which Anglican clergy often encounter.

The Joint Working Group, GTUM, and the *Ecumenical Dimension in the Formation of Those Engaged in Pastoral Work* all commend the use of existing ecumenical agreed statements for the purposes of ecumenical formation—not just as a means of informing, but in the hopes that as future clergy become conversant with these texts and their implications, the chances for these agreements's reception in the most local expressions of the church will be enhanced. The four documents I have selected here were chosen because (1) the Anglican Church of Canada was in some way involved in the development of each agreement, and (explicitly or implicitly) has the church's sanction; (2) they each have the potential for a practical application to a congregational setting; (3) they each deal with concrete scenarios involving the ecclesial relationships that clergy are very likely to encounter in the course of their congregational ministries, something that both bishops and seminary heads surveyed flagged as important; (4) they are each relatively short and are all freely available online; and (5) they each point to underpinning pastoral and theological questions that might lead students with the interest and ability to engage with these ecumenical texts more deeply.

---

80. IARCCUM, *Growing Together*, §5.

The Modalities of the Course

Having laid out the primary sources for the content of such an overview course, consideration now needs to be given to the manner in which it would be delivered. What I will present is one possible vision of how this formation might be offered, recognizing that I am neither a pedagogue nor a specialist in course design. I begin with what I consider to be the realistic assumption that seminaries and theological colleges not already offering some form of course in ecumenics will continue to be unable or unwilling to do so, whatever the reasons. This starting point will necessarily direct how the course is delivered, who delivers it, and who the participants might be.

The method of delivery would be primarily online, through the use of webinars and possibly also online discussion groups. While an ecumenically and academically qualified Anglican primary instructor would oversee the course and serve as the participants's evaluator, suitable invited guests from other relevant Christian traditions could be incorporated into each of the units. This would provide both access to specialized knowledge regarding each ecumenical agreement being discussed and also provide denominational diversity to the discussions. So, for example, a suitable Lutheran academic could be invited to contribute to the webinar on the Waterloo Declaration. A Roman Catholic bishop conversant with *Growing Together in Unity and Mission* could address that document. There are currently scholars in the United Church, Lutheran, and Methodist traditions whose specialized research areas include ecumenical shared ministries. There is also no shortage of individuals who could speak to the ecumenical implications of recognizing a common baptism. An internet-based approach to the course would make access to such expertise both relatively easy and inexpensive.

Like Budde's proposal, this one assumes that the participants will belong to a single tradition, in this case the Anglican Church of Canada. While true that most everything we have discussed thus far has extolled the virtues of denominationally diverse learning cohorts, the primary target of the ecumenical ministerial formation discussed here has been Canadian Anglican clergy. The invited guests noted above would provide some ecumenical variety. Course assignments could also include a component that involves some kind of ecumenical engagement in the participant's local context that is germane to the texts being discussed.

Because it seems unlikely that the seminaries or theological colleges could be relied upon to implement such a course, I would recommend that leadership in providing this ecumenical ministerial formation come from

A Proposed Revised Practice

the national expression of the Anglican Church of Canada: the General Synod. Ecumenical relations and theological education are, historically and currently, two programmatic areas still in the purview of the General Synod. A 2010 national consultation on theological education raised the idea of the development of a "national faculty" of instructors from Anglican-affiliated institutions "to provide high-quality theological education in remote areas in time-sensitive and locally culturally appropriate programs."[81] There is no indication that the idea ever took any concrete form, but could it be adapted for the purposes of providing this ecumenical overview course? If faculty could not be enlisted, could Anglican seminaries or theological colleges which already have the digital infrastructure in place to provide such a web-based course contribute in that way? Could the General Synod's animator for ecumenical and interfaith relations play a leading role in the development, implementation, and delivery of this course? This would leverage that staff person's expertise and experience, the General Synod's mandate in this area, and a collective desire to see ecumenical reception in our church enhanced through ecumenical formation. It would also relieve the burden of offering such a course from seminaries or theological colleges lacking the will, incentive, or capacity to do so.

The overview course could be designed in such a way that it would meet the requirements demanded of a credit course so that students enrolled in, for example, an accredited master of divinity program could take the course as an elective toward the fulfilment of their degree. At the same time it could be more made more widely available to other individuals who are not seeking credits toward a degree but nevertheless wish to participate. This would not mean auditing the class in the usual sense, since these other participants would still be expected to complete the same (or a modified version of) the course requirements. Rather than academic credits, these participants might receive something like a "General Synod Certificate in Ecumenical Formation," or some other similar recognition for having successfully completed the overview course. Such a flexible approach and delivery method would also broaden the scope of possible students to include the increasing number of individuals preparing for ordination in schemes other than the traditional three-year MDiv track, such as through diocesan schools of ministry.

81. General Synod, *d'Youville Report*. Notably, the final report of this this three-day national gathering of the heads of Anglican seminaries and theological colleges and other constituencies concerned with theological education—including four ecumenical participants—made no mention of ecumenical ministerial formation.

Because the course would have these two streams—one for academic credit and another for the General Synod credential—the potential pool of participants would still further expand far beyond those in the midst of ministerial formation. It could therefore include current clergy, thereby potentially mitigating the large numbers of Anglican priests serving in Canada who received little or no explicit ecumenical formation during their theological education.

Incentives for those still preparing for ordination to take the course might include their sponsoring bishop making it a pre-ordination requirement, in the same many dioceses require their postulants to complete clinical pastoral education before being admitted to holy orders. Some dioceses require active clergy to complete a certain number of "continuing education credits" each year as a way of fostering ongoing professional development, and this course could be added to those awarding such credits. All stipendiary clergy in the Anglican Church of Canada have access to a national Continuing Education Plan, which helps offset the cost of courses such as this, thus providing a financial incentive to participate. When, how often, and over how long a period of time such a course would be offered would need to be negotiated according to factors like the requirements of external bodies such as affiliated universities or accrediting bodies. If the course were offered on a strictly non-credit basis, length, timing, format, and requirements would presumably be more flexible. There is also no reason why such a course could not also be open to permanent deacons (or those preparing for the vocational diaconate), as well as interested individuals who are not ordained or in the ordination stream.

It might also be worthwhile considering whether such a course could be offered jointly with the Evangelical Lutheran Church in Canada, including Lutheran candidates for ordination as well as current pastors and diaconal ministers expressing an interest. Such an effort would certainly be in the spirit of full communion's exhortation that the two churches do as much together as possible, and the Waterloo Declaration would itself form a key part of the curriculum. The ELCIC is also a participant in ecumenical shared ministries and the 1975 mutual recognition of baptism pact. Lutherans have their own history of separation and reconciliation with the Catholic Church, and so that section of the course could be easily adapted, perhaps drawing from the 2017 bilateral document *From Conflict to Communion*. Like *Growing Together in Unity and Mission*, it catalogues theological convergence between Lutherans and Catholics and points toward

A Proposed Revised Practice

its concrete implications, against the particular backdrop of the five hundredth anniversary of the Lutheran Reformation.

Admittedly, this proposed overview course does not fully embody the holistic approach envisioned by Budde. It satisfies the "inform" stage of her model in that it would ideally provide participants with a basic understanding of the theology, governance, worship, and culture of the other churches being encountered through the ecumenical agreements being studied. Less obvious is how the "form" and "transform" dimensions could be easily incorporated into such a course, particularly when it is intended to be delivered primarily online. Extracurricular activities characterize "form," and for the purposes of this course these could be translated into individual students experiencing a local ecumenical partner's worship, or attending a meeting of its decision-making body. "Transform" is supposed to be the stage naturally resulting from the previous two, in which the didactic and extracurricular ecumenical experiences of "inform" and "form" help the student integrate an ecumenical consciousness into their lives as Christians and, especially, as ordained church leaders. As observed earlier, this transformative experience often hinges on a disruptive encounter of some kind with an ecclesial "other," and so the designers of such an overview course would need to be creative in helping individual participants find opportunities to experience such an encounter within their local contexts, and also provide a means by which the students could both relate, process, and integrate that experience in such a way that it might have a positive outcome—an ecumenical change of heart, conversion, or transformation.

Even if such a fundamental reorientation does not occur within the confines of the overview course itself, the hope is that it will at least enhance the possibility for such in the future. Ecumenists have long lamented that the fate of many hard-won and painstakingly crafted ecumenical agreed statements is to sit on shelves gathering dust. This revised practice would pull back the cobwebs from four of these accords, drawing them to the attention of a new generation of clergy, and potentially breathe new life into them so that the visible Christian unity that they describe in their pages might find tangible expression in local communities.

Conclusion

THIS RESEARCH HAS ATTEMPTED to demonstrate that the form and content of a seminarian's ecumenical formation during their preparatory studies for ministry are determinative for the kinds of ecumenical attitudes and activities they will carry into their ordained ministries. After surveying and assessing the form and content of ecumenical formation currently being offered by the major centers of theological formation affiliated with the Anglican Church of Canada, both seem insufficient to the task of inculcating the kind of profound ecumenical consciousness the denomination's own official statements claim they seek in their clergy. In response, this research collated decades of experience and reflection—as well as drawing on the insights of transformative learning theory—to articulate an ideal and holistic method of ecumenical ministerial formation. A pragmatic revised practice was then proposed, one that admittedly falls short of this ideal method, since the prospects of implementing such a fulsome program of ecumenical ministerial formation in the current context are unpromising.

The contemporary challenges faced by theological colleges and seminaries mirror those being encountered by the mainline churches they are intended to serve: diminishing enrolment, financial limitations, increasing demands being placed on a shrinking number of people. Add to these a climate in which curricula are expected to equip future clergy to serve in a relatively new secularized context, and a general malaise in attitudes toward institution-centered ecumenism, it is perhaps unsurprising that ecumenical studies of any kind do not figure high (or at all) among the priorities of many institutions of theological education. Dowd's survey of Canada's theological colleges and seminaries in 1998 revealed only two of twenty-three respondents offered a specific course in ecumenism, neither compulsory. The explanation most frequently offered was a lack of capacity: "[M]any institutes reported that, while they would like to 'do' more in

Conclusion

this area, there simply were not the resources to accomplish the task."[1] This strain on capacities has, if anything, grown more acute in the two decades since. This is arguably as true for the students as it is for the institutions at which they study. Even in the 1980s a study of theological students suggested that the volume of courses required by their sponsoring church (or the college or seminary affiliated with that church) made a more ecumenically rounded formation difficult, with regrettable consequences: "[S]tudents can become so concerned about fulfilling the requirements mandated by their denomination for ordination that they fail to achieve any ecumenical perspective. In effect, one's own denominational vantage point becomes *the* standard for judging all other denominations; consequently, what is denominationally distinctive can easily become ecumenically divisive."[2]

The revised practice offered here, therefore, is one crafted in such a way that some form of it might actually stand a chance of being implemented in the current context. The alternative would be to simply join the earnest but futile chorus of unheeded calls for seminaries and theological colleges to implement more fulsome—and, admittedly, costly—forms of ecumenical formation.

There are other ways in which this research project has its limitations. For example, in chapter 4 I outlined some ways which, in retrospect, the survey questions could have been in some cases expanded and in other cases more precise, thus eliciting responses that might have pointed more clearly to a correlation between one's ministerial formation and their subsequent ecumenical consciousness and engagement. Similarly, a clearer connection between transformative learning and ecumenical formation might have been more easily established had I engaged with that pedagogical theory earlier in my research.

The governing claim with which I began this research was that there exists a relationship between the manner and content of the formation of the clergy of Anglican Church of Canada and their subsequent knowledge of and commitment to ecumenism. While the results of the survey of clergy points to the veracity of that claim, there is insufficient data to draw an unbroken line between the model, setting, and content of one's ministerial formation and their subsequent ecumenical consciousness and engagement. At the conclusion of chapter 4, I attempted to address what I perceive, in retrospect, as some of the shortcomings of the survey itself, which may have

1. Dowd, "Ecumenical Education," 27.
2. Ford, "Ecumenical Commitment," 201.

led to this less-than-conclusive result. In addition, I note that it is also very likely that interviews with some of the respondents would elucidate their survey answers in such a way that might more clearly support my claim of a one-to-one relationship between a seminarian's ecumenical formation and their ecumenical disposition post-ordination.

Nevertheless, the subset of sixteen clergy whose responses manifested at least the hints of the kind of transformative ecumenical formation experience this research advocates does suggest there is a connection between the form and content of their theological education and their subsequent ecumenical attitudes and involvement. It is telling, for example, that every member of that subset studied with faculty and fellow students who were not Anglican, and all but two engaged in extracurricular and/or social activities with students of other Christian traditions. Also suggestive is that while just over two-thirds (67 percent) of the full sample of two hundred and six clergy indicated that their ministerial formation had changed their attitudes toward other Christian traditions, only sixteen (barely 8 percent) used language suggesting that this ecumenical attitudinal adjustment was substantial or significantly impacting their current ministries.

It must be also noted that some important voices are absent from this study. No clergy from the Anglican Church of Canada's two northernmost dioceses, Arctic and Yukon, responded to the survey.[3] Only one response was received from the Indigenous Spiritual Ministry of Mishamikoweesh, a self-determining Indigenous diocese straddling eastern Manitoba and northwestern Ontario. Indigenous Anglican clergy serving in other dioceses may have participated in the survey, but since respondents were not asked to identify themselves as Indigenous or non-Indigenous, this cannot be quantified.

Two factors—separately or together—may help explain this lack of participation. One is the so-called "digital divide." Nearly 20 percent of Canadians still do not have access to high-speed internet, and as a House of Commons committee recently reported, most of them live in rural and remote areas such as the North. Since this survey was delivered exclusively by electronic means, one possible explanation for the lack of response from Anglican clergy serving in Canada's most northern regions (be they

---

3. Mitigating this somewhat is the fact that the Arthur Turner Training School, the only Anglican centre for ministerial formation in the Far North, did participate in the survey of seminaries and theological colleges.

Conclusion

Indigenous or not) is that they simply lacked the sufficient technological means by which to receive or complete it.

A second possible explanation is a linguistic divide. The survey was made available exclusively in English. While this is the dominant (and functionally official) language of the Anglican Church of Canada, it is not the only tongue spoken by Canadian Anglicans. Inuktitut, for example, is the language of the majority of Anglicans in the Diocese of the Arctic, which encompasses the Northwest Territories, Nunavut, and the Nunavik region of northern Quebec. In Mishamikoweesh the primary languages spoken are Cree and Oji-Cree. Similarly, unilingual francophone Anglican clergy in Quebec may also have been unable to complete the survey because it was offered only in English.

This absence of perspectives on ecumenical formation from Indigenous Anglicans and from those in the Far North diminishes this study because the search for the church's visible unity is unique in these contexts—in part because of the enduring and damaging legacy of colonialism, and also because of the realities that come with living in remote regions that are typically underserved, frequently impoverished, and climactically harsh.

Through what he called "a little bit of spiritual physics," National Indigenous Anglican Bishop Mark MacDonald attempted to relate something of these contexts in an address to the 2013 Assembly of the World Council of Churches in Busan, South Korea: "At fifty below zero, denominational differences disappear. And there's an important lesson to be found in that. This does not mean that things go 'mushy.' It just means that in the context of human need—when disunity is a luxury you can't afford—you begin to recognize the deeper unity that you have in Christ."[4]

Another ecumenical reality particular to Indigenous contexts—one shared with other colonized peoples in many parts of the world—is the legacy of European missionaries having introduced not only Christianity to the First Peoples they encountered, but also "foreign-made divisions between the churches."[5] Indigenous communities that enjoyed relative unity and cohesiveness before contact with Christian colonizers became fractured as they evangelized and divided along denominational lines. These breaches in Indigenous communities have endured, long after the missionaries who introduced them have moved on.

---

4. MacDonald, "Unity Plenary."
5. Starkloff, "Theology and Aboriginal Religion," 319.

Formation for Transformation

This study also does not include the voices of the laity. As explained early on, this research chose deliberately to focus on the ecumenical formation of clergy. However, this choice was born not out of some form of clericalism, but rather because of the specific role the ordained play in the teaching and formation of the laypeople they serve. If deacons, priests, and bishops do not model ecumenical attitudes and actions, it is unlikely the laity who look to them for guidance will either. Nevertheless, one possible avenue for future research in this field is the ecumenical formation of Canadian Anglican laity, perhaps attempting to draw a correlation between the ecumenical attitudes and activities of their pastors and their own.

Another possible pathway for future research on ecumenical ministerial formation would be to engage with intergroup contact theory. First developed in the 1950s, this social psychological theory suggests that under the right conditions, face-to-face contact between individuals belonging to different and clearly defined groups reduces prejudice. Such a method resonates strongly with the kind of holistic ecumenical ministerial formation commended throughout this book. While intergroup contact theory was initially developed to address racial and ethnic prejudices, subsequent research has seen it applied to a variety of target groups.[6] Using theological students from different traditions as target groups would be one way of applying intergroup contact theory to the study of ecumenical ministerial formation. Something close to this was undertaken in a study of how the racial attitudes of theological students were changed through participation in the ecumenical Student Interracial Ministry program at New York's Union Theological Seminary in the 1960s.[7] That research brought together intergroup contact theory and transformative learning theory to show how an intensive, in-person program exposing participants to disorienting difference through sustained encounter with people of other racially distinct groups can result in a permanent and positive changed perspective in attitude toward another group. A focussed application of intergroup contact theory to ecumenical ministerial formation—perhaps also in conversation with transformative learning theory—merits pursuit.

What is the cost of the task of ecumenical ministerial formation failing to be accomplished? One practical outcome is that as theological colleges and seminaries have lost the will and/or capacity to privilege ecumenical formation, a generation of clergy are now serving in positions of leadership

---

6. Pettigrew and Tropp, "A Meta-Analytic Test of Intergroup Contact Theory," 762.
7. Moll, "Theological Education in Action."

in the churches with little or no exposure to the ecumenical movement, its principles or imperatives, or to the theology, worship, and adherents of other ecclesial traditions. One U.S. ecumenist has observed, "Many ecumenical leaders have complained rightly that American seminaries have been educating generations of ecumenically illiterate clergy, and that the [ecumenical] movement has been paying the price."[8] The World Council of Churches has expressed the same sense of urgency on a still wider level:

> There is no future for the ecumenical movement as a whole if there is no commitment to ecumenical formation processes in formal and non-formal theological education programs of WCC member churches. If theological education fails to be guided by an ecumenical vision of a church renewed in mission and service to the whole of humankind, there will be a serious shortage in terms of a new generation of Christian leaders, pastors, and theological teachers carrying on the ecumenical vision and commitment into the twenty-first century, and a widening gap and estrangement between the majority clergy and ever fewer experts on the ecumenical movement and ecumenical theological discourse which can already be observed in a number of member churches.[9]

Anglican ecumenist and ecclesiologist Paul Avis also draws this inextricable link between unity and mission, one that is forgotten at our peril: "Mission pursued without a care for unity is divorced from an essential attribute of the church and in danger of descending into mere pragmatism. But, on the other hand, to be credible in today's climate, the cause of unity must be explicitly linked to the cause of mission."[10]

Others argue that the price for institutional negligence in ecumenical ministerial formation is still greater than just compromising the effectiveness or credibility of the churches's participation in God's mission. In its 2005 report, the Joint Working Group between the Catholic Church and the WCC lamented that "a new generation of Christians is sometimes unaware of the way things were and how much things have changed in the decades since the founding of the WCC and since the Second Vatican Council."[11] No mere expression of ecumenical nostalgia, the report expresses an anxiety shared by many in the movement that a failure to adequately educate

---

8. Kessler, "Head Change," 4.
9. World Council of Churches, "Ecumenical Covenant," §III.
10. Avis, *Reshaping Ecumenical Theology*, 23.
11. Joint Working Group, *Eighth Report*, §V.2.

the faithful about "the way things were" risks a return to a time in which fear, ignorance, mistrust, suspicion, stereotypes, caricatures, recrimination, anathematization—even persecution—characterized the relations between divided churches. Even if the movement toward the restoration of the full visible unity of the church is taking much longer than first hoped during the heyday of the ecumenical movement in the last century, the progress made in promoting healing and rapprochement between separated churches is nevertheless remarkable.

That gift and achievement is at risk, however, and could give way to a retrenchment back into denominationalism, even in the realm of ministerial formation: "The single most remarkable trend . . . in world Christianity is that the degree of denominational fragmentation in the international and regional landscape of theological education networks and institutions is as high as never before in the history of Christianity."[12] Among the by-products of this renewed denominational fragmentation and retrenchment are ethnocentrism, fundamentalism, and religiously sanctioned nationalism. This trend at one time seemed more prevalent in some regions of the Global South, a particular cause for concern as Christianity's center of gravity moves steadily in that direction. However, in recent years there is evidence of such trends closer to home as well. In a world increasingly gripped by nationalism, regional conflicts with global dimensions, mass migration, xenophobia, climate change, and the still-unfolding consequences of the COVID-19 pandemic, the church's visible and tangible witness is compromised by disunity. The former general secretary of the World Council of Churches, Olav Fyske Tveit, once put it this way, riffing off of Archbishop Desmond Tutu's assertion in that apartheid was too big for the divided churches of South Africa to challenge individually: "The needs of the world for reconciliation with God, with one another, and with nature are too big for a divided church."[13]

The final pages of this book were written in the midst of the COVID-19 pandemic, a phenomenon that resulted in entire countries going into a form of quarantine for several consecutive weeks (or sometimes months) in hopes of stymying the spread of the virus. Two specific aspects of the pandemic's outworkings are germane to this research. One involves the exclusive shift to online learning made by many post-secondary institutions—including seminaries and theological colleges—in the days immediately following

---

12. Werner, "Unfinished Agenda," 12.
13. Tveit, "Greetings."

Conclusion

the government-ordered closure of indoor gatherings. Almost overnight, online course offerings became normative. In chapter 5, I outlined some of the limitations of web-based learning, particularly for the kind of ecumenical formation that seeks to create the conditions for a transformative learning experience. Nevertheless, that so many institutions and students have rapidly embraced online teaching (albeit out of necessity) potentially bodes well for the implementation of my proposed revised practice. The financial impact of the pandemic on post-secondary institutions also further reduces the chances than anything other than an online proposal for enhanced ecumenical formation would be taken up.

It is this economic dimension of COVID-19's consequences that is the other element relevant to this study, and to ecumenism in general. Churches of every tradition have been hard hit by the pandemic, which resulted in the suspension of public worship and therefore several successive Sundays without financial offerings from parishioners. Local, regional, and national expressions of the church in Canada—some of which were already facing financial uncertainty before the coronavirus—may find recovery from the pandemic difficult or impossible. It was noted in chapter 5 that sometimes economic hardship is one of the drivers for the creation of ecumenical shared ministries at the local level. It may be that the lasting economic impact of the COVID-19 pandemic results in more ecumenical collaboration at the congregational level, but perhaps also at the diocesan and national levels. As one survey respondent stated (pre-pandemic): "I think it will be more and more necessary to have joint projects and ministries in the future as some denominations [continue] to decline." COVID-19 and its consequences may be accelerating this decline and, in turn, accelerating ecumenical collaboration out of necessity.

As noted earlier, the progress of this research was retarded in terms of time and scope by my election to the Anglican episcopate two years after I had begun the doctor of ministry program of which this study was a part. This resulted—or so I initially thought—in my removal from a vocational context that was almost fully oriented toward the content of this research (that of a national ecumenical officer) to one that seemingly included ecumenism as one of countless aspects of ministry. However, I quickly realized that thinking in such terms was to succumb to the distorted understanding of ecumenism that Pope John Paul II warned about in the quotation from *Ut Unum Sint* that begins this book. Ecumenism is not an appendix to the church's life and work, but rather imbues every aspect of its mission.

Formation for Transformation

I therefore prefer to see the vocational shift that took place in the midst of this research as a unique opportunity to try and implement some of the ecumenical best practices that have been highlighted in this research. As a member of the General Synod staff, my capacities in this respect were limited to informing, encouraging, and cajoling. As a bishop I have more latitude to be appropriately directive in applying the fruits of this research in the diocese I serve, and potentially beyond. And so, if nothing else, this research will have better equipped me for my own ongoing ministry as an agent of ecumenical reception—and will potentially also help equip the next nimble generation of ecumenical log drivers.

Bibliography

Alfeyev, Hilarion. "The Reception of the Ecumenical Councils in the Early Church." *St. Vladimir's Theological Quarterly* 47, no. 3-4 (2003): 413-30.
Amirthan, Sam and Cyris H.S. Moon, eds. *The Teaching of Ecumenics*. Geneva: WCC, 1987.
Amos, Clare. "Theological Education in the Anglican Communion." In *Handbook of Theological Education in World Christianity*, edited by Dietrich Werner, David Esterline, Namsoon Kang and Joshva Raja, 641-51. Eugene, OR: Wipf & Stock, 2010.
Anglican Consultative Council. "B17:04 Reception of Ecumenical Texts in the Anglican Communion." https://www.anglicancommunion.org/structures/instruments-of-communion/acc/acc-17/resolutions.aspx.
Anglican-Roman Catholic International Commission. *The Final Report*. Cincinnati: Forward Movement, 1982.
Anokwulu, Sebastian Chukwuma. *The Ecumenical Imperative and Formation of Ecumenical Consciousness among Pastoral Workers*. Bloomington, IN: Trafford, 2013.
Association of Theological Schools. "Accredited Schools Offering Six or More Courses Online." https://staging.ats.edu/member-schools/member-school-distance-education.
———. "Educational Models and Practices in Theological Education Peer Group Final Reports." https://www.ats.edu/uploads/resources/current-initiatives/ educational-models/publications-and-presentations/peer-group-final-reports/peer-group-final-report-book.pdf.
———. "Petition for Comprehensive Distance Education Approval." https://ats.edu/uploads/accrediting/documents/petition-comprehensive-distance-education%20 170207.docx.
Avis, Paul. "Are We Receiving 'Receptive Ecumenism'?" *Ecclesiology* 8 (2012): 223-34.
———. *Becoming a Bishop: A Theological Handbook of Episcopal Ministry*. London: Bloomsbury T&T Clark, 2015.
———. *Reshaping Ecumenical Theology: The Church Made Whole?* London: T & T Clark, 2010.
———, ed. *Seeking the Truth of Change in the Church: Reception, Communion and the Ordination of Women*. London: T & T Clarke, 2004.
Bates, Tony. "A National Survey of University Online and Distance Learning in Canada." Online Learning and Distance Education Resources. https://www.tonybates.ca/ 2016/03/23/a-national-survey-of-university-online-and-distance-learning-in-canada.

Bibliography

Beardsall, Sandra, Mitzi J. Budde and William P. McDonald. *Daring to Share: Multi-Denominational Congregations in the United States and Canada*. Eugene, OR: Pickwick, 2018.

———. "Space for the Other: Ecumenical Shared Ministries." *Journal of Ecumenical Studies* 54, no. 2 (Spring 2019): 151–67.

Becker, Ulrich. "Ecumenical Formation." In *A History of the Ecumenical Movement, Vol. 3, 1968–2000*, edited by John Briggs, Mercy Amba Oduyoye and Georges Tsetis, 175–93. Geneva: WCC, 2004.

Best, Thomas F., Lorelei F. Fuchs, et. al. eds. *Growth in Agreement IV: International Dialogue Texts and Agreed Statements, 2004–2014* (two volumes). Geneva: WCC, 2017.

Bevans, Stephen B. *Models of Contextual Theology*. Maryknoll, NY: Orbis, 2002.

Bliss, Frederick M. *Understanding Reception: A Backdrop to Its Ecumenical Use*. Milwaukee: Marquette University Press, 1993.

Booth, Wayne C., Gregory G. Colomb and Joseph M. Williams, eds. *The Craft of Research*. 2nd ed. Chicago: University of Chicago Press, 2008.

Browning, Don S. *A Fundamental Practical Theology: Descriptive and Strategic Proposals*. Minneapolis, MN: Fortress, 1991.

Brownlee, Kelly, ed. *A Place to Remember: The Ecumenical Institute at Bossey*. Geneva: WCC, 2013.

Buchanan, Colin. *Did Anglicans and Roman Catholics Agree on the Eucharist? A Revisit of the Anglican-Roman Catholic International Commission's Agreed Statements of 1971 and Related Documents*. Eugene, OR: Pickwick, 2018.

Budde, Mitzi J. "Ecumenical Formation in Denominational Theological Seminaries." DMin diss., Wesley Theological Seminary, 2004.

———. "The Vocation for Unity in Theological Education." In *Staying Open, Remaining One: Educating Leaders for a 21st-Century Church*, edited by Richard J. Jones and J. Barney Hawkins IV, 98–108. New York: Morehouse, 2010.

Butler, Perry. "The History of Anglicanism: From the Eighteenth Century to the Present Day." In *The Study of Anglicanism*, edited by Stephen Sykes, John Booty and Jonathan Knight, 30–51. London: SPCK, 1998.

Canadian Conference of Catholic Bishops and the House of Bishops of the Anglican Church of Canada. *Pastoral Guidelines for Interchurch Marriages between Anglicans and Roman Catholics in Canada*. Ottawa: CCCB, 1987.

Clifford, Catherine. "A Wake Up Call: Ecumenical Formation for All." *Ecumenism* 133 (March 1999): 14–19.

Commission on Faith and Order. *Baptism, Eucharist and Ministry*. Geneva: WCC, 1982.

———. *The Church: Towards a Common Vision*. Geneva: WCC, 2013.

Commission on Faith and Witness. *Initiation into Christ: Common Teaching and Ecumenical Reflections on Preparation for Baptism*. Toronto: Canadian Council of Churches, 1991.

Congar, Yves. "La « réception » comme réalité ecclésiologique." *Revue des Sciences philosophiques et théologiques* 56 (1972): 369–403.

Delloff, Linda-Marie. "Embracing Estrangement." *Theological Education* 34 (Supplement, Autumn 1997): 15–22.

Denaux, Adelbert, Nicholas Sagovsky, et. al. eds. *Looking Towards a Church Fully Reconciled: The Final Report of the Anglican-Roman Catholic International Commission, 1983–2005 (ARCIC II)*. London: SPCK, 2016.

Bibliography

Dowd, Thomas. "Ecumenical Education in Canada: A Survey." *Ecumenism* 133 (March 1999): 24–27.

Ecumenical Patriarchate of Constantinople. "'Unto the Churches of Christ Everywhere,' Encyclical of the Ecumenical Patriarchate, 1920." https://www.oikoumene.org/resources/documents/unto-the-churches-of-christ-everywhere-encyclical-of-the-ecumenical-patriarchate-1920.

Ecumenical Shared Ministries Task Force. *Ecumenical Shared Ministries Handbook*. http://www.anglican.ca/wp-content/uploads/2010/10/Ecumenical-Shared-Ministries-Handbook.pdf.

Episcopal Church. "An Agreement of Full Communion—Called to Common Mission." https://www.episcopalchurch.org/ministries/ecumenical-interreligious/agreement-of-full-communion-called-to-common-mission.

Erickson, John H. and Eileen W. Lindner. "Worship and Prayer in Ecumenical Formation." *Theological Education* 34 (Supplement, Autumn 1997): 23–30.

Faith and Order Secretariat. *Reports of the World Conference on Faith and Order: Lausanne, Switzerland, August 3–21, 1927*. Boston: Faith and Order Secretariat, 1928.

Flannery, Austin, ed. *Vatican Council II: Constitutions, Decrees, Declarations*. Northport, NY: Costello, 1996.

Flynn, Kevin. "Ecumenical Dialogue and Formation for Ministry." *Ecumenism* 182 (Summer 2011): 3–5.

Freire, Paulo. *Pedagogy of the Oppressed*. 30th anniversary ed. New York: Continuum, 2000.

Gardner, Matt. "Challenges draw Trinity and Wycliffe closer." *Anglican Journal*. https://www.anglicanjournal.com/challenges-draw-trinity-and-wycliffe-closer.

Gassman, Günther. "From Reception to Unity: The History and Ecumenical Significance of the Concept of Reception." In *Community, Unity, Communion: Essays in Honour of Mary Tanner*, edited by Colin Podmore, 117–29. London: Church House, 1998.

Geernaert, Donna. "Reception: A Canadian Perspective." In *Faith and Order in Moshi: The 1996 Commission Meeting*, edited by Alan Falconer, 86–95. Geneva: WCC, 1998.

General Synod of the Anglican Church of Canada. *Anglican Church Directory 2017*. Toronto: ABC, 2017.

———. "Anglican-Lutheran Guidelines for Clergy Serving in Each Other's Churches." https://www.anglican.ca/faith/eir/full-communion-partnership/a-l-clergy-guidelines.

———. "Bilateral Dialogues." https://www.anglican.ca/faith/eir/dialogues.

———. *Competencies for Ordination to the Priesthood in the Anglican Church of Canada*. https://www.anglican.ca/faith/ministry/education/competencies-priesthood.

———. "Towards a Renewed Ecumenical Strategy." https://gs2004.anglican.ca/atsynod/reports/003-10.htm.

———. *Vision 2019: A Plan for the Anglican Church of Canada*. http://archive.anglican.ca/gs2010/wp-content/uploads/019-GS2010-Vision-2019-Report-and-Appendices.pdf.

———. "Waterloo Ministries Directory." https://www.anglican.ca/resources/waterloo-ministries-directory.

———. *The d'Youville Report: National Gathering on Theological Education, January 2010*. https://www.anglican.ca/wp-content/uploads/2010/02/dYouville-Report.pdf.

Gilligan, Michael. "Does What Is Taught at Bossey Equal What is Learned?" *Theological Education* 34 (Supplement, Autumn 1997): 39–46.

Graham, Elaine, Heather Walton and Frances Ward. *Theological Reflection: Methods*. London: SCM, 2005.

Bibliography

Gros, Jeffrey, Thomas F. Best, et. al. eds. *Growth in Agreement III: International Dialogue Texts and Agreed Statements, 1998-2005*. Geneva: WCC, 2007.

Gros, Jeffrey, Rozanne Elder, et. al. eds. *Common Witness to the Gospel: Documents on Anglican-Roman Catholic Relations, 1983-1995*. Washington: United States Catholic Conference, 1997.

Gros, Jeffrey, Harding Meyer, et. al. eds. *Growth in Agreement II: Reports and Agreed Statements of Ecumenical Conversations on a World Level, 1992-1998*. Geneva: WCC, 2001.

Hadsell, Heidi. "Two Agendas for Ecumenical Formation." *Theological Education* 34 (Supplement, Autumn 1997): 47-54.

Hadsell, Heidi and John B. Lindner. "Bossey's Ecumenical Formation: A Methodology for a Pluralistic Age." *Ecumenism* 133 (March 1999): 8-10.

Handy, Robert T. "Trends in Canadian and American Theological Education, 1880-980." *Theological Education* 18, no. 2 (Spring 1982): 175-218.

Harding, Thomas. "The Churches' Council of Theological Education in Canada: A Model for Ecumenical Co-operation." *Ecumenism* 133 (March 1999): 28-32.

Hayes, Alan L. "The Anglican Church of Canada." In *The Wiley-Blackwell Companion to the Anglican Communion*, edited by Ian S. Markham, J. Barney Hawkins IV, Justyn Terry and Leslie Nuñez, 475-88. Chichester, UK: John Wiley & Sons, 2013.

———. *Anglicans in Canada: Controversies and Identity in Historical Perspective*. Chicago: University of Illinois Press, 2004.

———. "The Toronto School of Theology." University of Toronto (UTORweb). http://individual.utoronto.ca/hayes/xty_canada/tsthistory.html.

Henn, William. "Reflections on Ecumenical Reception." In *Faith and Order in Moshi: The 1996 Commission Meeting*, edited by Alan Falconer, 79-85. Geneva: WCC, 1998.

Hodgson, Jim. "Ecumenical Education and the Canadian Council of Churches." *Ecumenism* 113 (March 1994): 23.

Hughson, Thomas. "Beyond Ecumenical Dialogue." One in Christ 46, no. 1 (2012): 24-37.

International Anglican-Roman Catholic Commission on Unity and Mission. *Growing Together in Unity and Mission: Building on 40 Years of Anglican-Roman Catholic Dialogue*. London: SPCK, 2007.

Jennings, Paul and Bruce Myers. "Background and Reflections on the Policy Regarding Authorized Lay Ministries of the Evangelical Lutheran Church in Canada." Anglican Church of Canada. https://www.anglican.ca/wp-content/uploads/Brief-on-ELCIC-Authorized-Lay-Ministries.pdf.

Joint Declaration on the Doctrine of Justification. Grand Rapids, MI: Eerdmans, 2000.

Joint Working Group between the Roman Catholic Church and the World Council of Churches. "Ecumenical Formation." In *The Ecumenical Movement: An Anthology of Key Texts and Voices*, edited by Michael Kinnamon and Brian E. Cope, 449-53. Geneva: WCC, 1997.

———. *Eighth Report*. Geneva: WCC, 2005.

———. "Fifth Report of Joint Working Group between the Roman Catholic Church and the World Council of Churches." In *The Ecumenical Review* 35:2 (April 1983): 215.

———. "Joint Working Group between the Roman Catholic Church and the World Council of Churches: First Official Report." In *The Ecumenical Review* 18:2 (April 1966): 244.

———. *Ninth Report*. Geneva: WCC, 2012.

———. *Reception: A Key to Ecumenical Progress*. Geneva: WCC, 2004.

Bibliography

———. *Seventh Report*. Geneva: WCC, 1998.
Kaempf, Bernard. "Réception et evolution de la théologie pratique dans le protestantisme." In *Précis de théologie pratique*, edited by Gilles Routhier and Marcel Viau, 9–25. Brussels: Lumen Vitae, 2007.
Kasper, Walter. *A Handbook of Spiritual Ecumenism*. Hyde Park, NY: New City, 2007.
———. *Harvesting the Fruits: Basic Aspects of Christian Faith in Ecumenical Dialogue*. London: Continuum, 2009.
Kessler, Diane C. "Head Change and Heart Work: Some Hopeful Signs in Ecumenical Formation." *Ecumenism* 133 (March 1999): 4–7.
Kilmartin, Edward J. "Reception in History: An Ecclesiological Phenomenon and its Significance." *Journal of Ecumenical Studies* 21, no. 1 (Winter 1984): 34–54.
Kinnamon, Michael. *Can a Renewal Movement Be Renewed? Questions for the Future of Ecumenism*. Grand Rapids, MI: Eerdmans, 2014.
———. "Ecumenical Formation in Seminaries." *Ecumenism* 133 (March 1999): 11–13.
Knowles, Norman, ed. *Seeds Scattered and Sown: Studies in the History of Canadian Anglicanism*. Toronto: ABC, 2008.
Kreiger, F.G., G.E. MacDermid and T.A. Mabey. "Atlantic School of Theology: An Environment of Ecumenical Formation for Ministry." *Ecumenism* 133 (March 1999): 33–36.
Leggett, Richard, ed. *A Companion to the Waterloo Declaration: Commentary and Essays on Lutheran-Anglican Relations in Canada*. Toronto: ABC, 1999.
Lindner, John B. and Linda-Marie Delloff. "The U.S. Bossey Assessment Project: An Introduction." *Theological Education* 34 (Supplement, Autumn 1997): 1–6.
Loder, James E. *The Transforming Moment*. 2nd ed. Colorado Springs, CO: Helmers & Howard, 1998.
Lutheran World Federation and Pontifical Council for Promoting Christian Unity. "Joint Statement by the Lutheran World Federation and the Pontifical Council for Promoting Christian Unity on the conclusion of the year of the common commemoration of the Reformation, 31st October 2017." https://press.vatican.va/content/salastampa/en/bollettino/pubblico/2017/10/31/171031a.pdf.
MacDonald, Mark. "Unity Plenary, WCC 10th Assembly, 5 November 2013." World Council of Churches. Video, 1:19:20. http://wcc2013.info/en/news-media/video/recordings/unity-plenary-wcc-10th-assembly-4-november-2013.html.
Mannion, Gerard. "Assisi 2012—Where We Dwell in Common: Pathways for Dialogue in the 21st Century." *One in Christ* 46, no. 1 (2012): 146–52.
McCullum, Hugh. *Radical Compassion: The Life and Times of Archbishop Ted Scott*. Toronto: ABC, 2004.
McIntire, C.T. "Unity among Many: The Formation of the United Church of Canada, 1899–1930." In *A History of the United Church of Canada*, edited by Don Schweitzer, 3–37. Waterloo, ON: Wilfred Laurier University Press, 2012.
Meyer, Harding and Lukas Vischer, eds. *Growth in Agreement I: Reports and Agreed Statements of Ecumenical Conversations on a World Level*. Geneva: WCC, 1984.
Mezirow, Jack and Associates. *Learning as Transformation: Critical Perspectives on a Theory in Progress*. San Francisco: Jossey-Bass, 2000.
Mezirow, Jack. "Transforming Learning: Theory to Practice." *New Directions for Adult and Continuing Education* 74 (Summer 1997): 5–12.
Minear, Paul S. "The Import of Ecumenical Developments for Theological Education—A Protestant View." *Theological Education* 3, no. 2 (Winter 1967): 308–16.

Bibliography

Moll, Kirk A. "Theological Education in Action: A Study of Racial Perspective Change among Participants in the Student Interracial Ministry of Union Theological Seminary (1960-968). Paper presented at the *Adult Education Research Conference*, Toronto, ON, 2011. https://newprairiepress.org/aerc/2011/papers/69.

Moltmann, Jürgen. "What Kind of Unity? The Dialogue Between the Traditions of East and West." In *Lausanne 77: Fifty Years of Faith and Order*, 38-47. Geneva: WCC, 1977.

Murray, K.D., ed. *From a Long Perspective: The Foundational Documents, Ecumenical Covenants, and Other Significant Agreements of the Anglican Church of Canada.* Toronto: ABC, 2007.

Murray. Paul D. "ARCIC III: Recognizing the Need for an Ecumenical Gear Change." *One in Christ* 45, no. 2 (Winter 2011): 200-211.

———. "In Search of a Way." In *The Oxford Handbook of Ecumenical Studies*. Oxford Handbooks Online. https://www.oxfordhandbooks.com/view/10.1093/oxfordhb/9780199600847.001.0001/oxfordhb-9780199600847-e-45.

———, ed., *Receptive Ecumenism and the Call to Catholic Learning: Exploring a Way for Contemporary Ecumenism.* Oxford: Oxford University Press, 2008.

Myers, Bruce. "A Gift Yet to Be Received: Presbyteral Confirmation and Anglican-Lutheran Relations in Canada." In *Journal of Ecumenical Studies* 49, no. 3 (Summer 2014): 458-80.

———. "John Simons: A Teacher of Anglicanism with an Ecumenical Spirit." In *Pro Christo et Ecclesia.* (Summer 2015): 6-7. http://dio-mdtc.ca/th_gallery/pro-christo-et-ecclesia-summer-2015/.

Naidoo, Marilyn. "Ministerial Formation of Theological Students through Distance Education." *HTS Teologiese Studies/Theological Studies* 68, no. 2 (June 2012): 1-8.

Nazir-Ali, Michael. "The Anglican Communion and Ecumenical Relations." In *The Wiley-Blackwell Companion to the Anglican Communion*, edited by Ian S. Markham, J. Barney Hawkins IV, Justyn Terry and Leslie Nuñez, 569-85. Chichester, UK: John Wiley & Sons, 2013.

Nichols, Mark. "The Formational Experiences of On-campus and Theological Distance Education Students." *Journal of Adult Theological Education* 13, no. 1 (May 2016): 18-32.

Nichols, Mark and Dewerse, Rosemary. "Evaluating Transformative Learning in Theological Education: A Mult-faceted Approach." *Journal of Adult Theological Education* 7, no. 1 (2010): 44-59.

Nissiotis, Nikos A. "The Meaning of Reception in Relation to the Results of Ecumenical Dialogue on the Basis of the Faith and Order Document *Baptism, Eucharist and Ministry*." *Greek Orthodox Theological Review* 30, no. 2 (1985): 147-74.

O'Gara, Margaret. "Formation for Transformation: The Ecumenical Directory Sets a Big Agenda." *Ecumenism* 117 (March 1995): 23-26.

———. *No Turning Back: The Future of Ecumenism*, edited by Michael Vertin. Collegeville, MN: Liturgical, 2014.

———. "The Theological Significance of Friendship in the Ecumenical Movement." In *That the World May Believe: Essays on Mission and Unity in Honour of George Vandervelde*, edited by Michael W. Goheen and Margaret O'Gara, 125-232. Landham, MD: University Press of America, 2006.

Ortega, Ofelia. "Contextuality and Community: Challenges for Theological Education and Ecumenical Formation." *International Review of Mission* 98, no. 1 (April 2009): 25-36.

Osmer, Richard R. *Practical Theology: An Introduction.* Grand Rapids, MI: Eerdmans, 2008.

Bibliography

Oxley, Simon. *Creative Ecumenical Education: Learning from One Another.* Geneva: WCC, 2002.

Pettigrew, Thomas F. and Linda R. Tropp. "A Meta-Analytic Test of Intergroup Contact Theory." *Journal of Personality and Social Psychology* 90, no. 5 (2006): 751–83.

Pobee, John, ed. *Towards Viable Theological Education: Ecumenical Imperative, Catalyst of Renewal.* Geneva: WCC, 1997.

Pontifical Council for Promoting Christian Unity. *Directory for the Application of Principals and Norms on Ecumenism.* Vatican City: PCPCU, 1993.

———. *The Ecumenical Dimension in the Formation of Those Engaged in Pastoral Work.* Vatican City: PCPCU, 1995. Accessed January 8, 2015.

Pope Paul VI and Archbishop Michael Ramsay. "Common Declaration." https://www.anglicancommunion.org/media/105816/Common-Declaration-March-1966.pdf.

Prairie Centre for Ecumenism. "Ecumenical Shared Ministries." https://pcecumenism.ca/ecumenical-shared-ministries.

Raiser, Konrad. "Fifty Years of Ecumenical Formation: Where Are We Going?" *The Ecumenical Review* 48, no. 4 (October 1996): 440–451.

———. "The Importance of the Ecumenical Vision for Theological Education and Ministerial Formation." *Ministerial Formation* 110 (April 2008): 77–81.

Rausch, Thomas P. "Reception: A Matter of Perception." *Ecumenical Trends* 15 (December 1986): 190–91.

———. "Reception Past and Present." *Theological Studies* 47, no. 3 (Spring 1986): 497–508.

Rawlyk, George A. *The Canadian Protestant Experience, 1760–1990.* Montreal: McGill-Queen's University Press, 1990.

Ray, William J. *Methods: Toward a Science of Behavior and Experience.* 10th ed. Belmont, CA: Wadsworth, 2012.

Reissner, Anne. "An Examination of Formational and Transformational Issues in Conducting Distance Learning, including Issues Related to Faculty Development." *Theological Education* 36, no. 1 (1999): 87–100.

Routhier, Gilles. "La « réception » : Histoire du thème et usage du concept," 15–65. In *La réception d'un concile.* Paris: Cerf, 1993.

Rowland-Jones, Sarah, ed. *The Vision Before Us: The Kyoto Report of the Inter-Anglican Standing Commission on Ecumenical Relations, 2000–2008.* London: Anglican Communion Office, 2009.

Rusch, William G. "*Baptism, Eucharist and Ministry*—and Reception." *Journal of Ecumenical Studies* 21, no. 1 (Winter 1984): 129–43.

———. *Ecumenical Reception: Its Challenge and Opportunity.* Grand Rapids, MI: Eerdmans, 2007.

Ryan, Thomas. *Christian Unity: How You Can Make a Difference.* New York: Paulist, 2015.

———. "Reception: Unpacking the New Holy Word," *Ecumenism* 72 (December 1983): 27–34.

———. *Tales of Christian Unity: The Adventures of an Ecumenical Pilgrim.* New York: Paulist, 1983.

Saint Paul University. "Master of Divinity." https://ustpaul.ca/program/master-of-divinity-anglican-studies-264.htm.

Sorenson, Christine Alison. "Formation, Transformative Learning, and Theological Education." PhD diss., University of Aukland, 2007. https://researchspace.auckland.ac.nz/handle/2292/2127.

Bibliography

Spencer, Leon P. "Theological Education in the Anglican Communion." In *The Wiley-Blackwell Companion to the Anglican Communion*, edited by Ian S. Markham, J. Barney Hawkins IV, Justyn Terry and Leslie Nuñez, 643–56. Chichester, UK: John Wiley & Sons, 2013.

Starkloff, Karl F. "Theology and Aboriginal Religion: Continuing the 'Wider Ecumenism.'" *Theological Studies* 68 (2007): 287–319.

Swinton, John and Harriet Mowat. *Practical Theology and Qualitative Research.* London: SCM Press, 2006.

Tanner, Mary. "The Ecumenical Future." In *The Study of Anglicanism*, edited by Stephen Sykes, John Booty and Jonathan Knight, 427–46. London: SPCK, 1998.

———. "Receiving Ecumenical Documents: The Four Rs of Reception." *One in Christ* 48, no. 1 (2014): 69–84.

Tanner, Tom. "Online learning at ATS schools: Part 1—Looking back at our past." Association of Theological Schools. https://www.ats.edu/uploads/resources/publications-presentations/colloquy-online/online-learning-part-1.pdf.

Tillard, Jean-Marie Roger. "Fondements ecclésiologiques de la 'réception' œcuménique." *Toronto Journal of Theology* 3, no. 1 (Spring 1987): 28–40.

Tite, Philip J. On the Necessity of Crisis: A Reflection on Pedagogical Conflict and the Academic Study of Religion." *Teaching Theology and Religion* 6, no. 2 (2003): 76–84.

Together in Mission and Ministry: The Porvoo Common Statement with Essays on Church and Ministry in Northern Europe. London: Church House, 1993.

Tveit, Olav Fykse. "Greetings to the 3rd Lausanne Congress for World Evangelization." World Council of Churches. https://www.oikoumene.org/resources/documents/greetings-to-the-3rd-lausanne-congress-for-world-evangelization.

United Church of Canada. "Mending the World: An Ecumenical Vision for Healing and Reconciliation." https://united-church.ca/community-and-faith/welcome-united-church-canada/partners-mission/interfaith-relations.

Wainwright, Geoffrey. "One Baptism, One Church?" In *The Oxford Handbook of Sacramental Theology*, edited by Hans Boersma and Matthew Levering, 466–86. Oxford: Oxford University Press, 2015.

Walking Together on the Way: An Agreed Statement of the Anglican-Roman Catholic International Commission (ARCIC III). London: SPCK, 2018.

Weber, Hans-Ruedi. "A Laboratory for Ecumenical Life." *The Ecumenical Review* 48, no. 4 (October 1996): 435–39.

Werner, Dietrich, et. al. eds. *Handbook of Theological Education in World Christianity.* Eugene, OR: Wipf & Stock, 2010.

West, Morris. "Lund Principle." In *Dictionary of the Ecumenical Movement*, 2nd ed., edited by Nicholas Lossky, et. al., 714–15. Geneva: WCC, 2002.

———. "Magna Charta on Ecumenical Formation in Theological Education in the 21st Century: Ten Key Convictions." *International Review of Mission* 98, no. 388 (April 2009): 161–70.

Willebrands, Johannes. "The Ecumenical Dialogue and its Reception." *Bulletin Centro Pro Unione* 27 (Spring 1985): 3–8.

Wood, Beatrice Y. "Learning a Religious Tradition: Identity by Contrast." *Theological Education* 34 (Supplement, Autumn 1997): 31–38.

World Council of Churches. *Constitution and Rules of the World Council of Churches.* World Council of Churches, 2013. https://www.oikoumene.org/en/resources/documents/assembly/2013-busan/adopted-documents-statements/wcc-constitution-and-rules.

Bibliography

———. "EC 06. Developing Effective Leadership: Contextual Ecumenical Formation and Theological Education." In *Ecumenical Conversations: Reports, Affirmations and Challenges from the 10th Assembly*, 35–44. Geneva: WCC, 2014.

———. "Ecumenical Covenant on Theological Education." Public Statement of the Ecumenical Theological Education Accompaniment Group, Endorsed by the WCC Central Committee, March 17, 2012. https://www.oikoumene.org/en/resources/documents/wcc-programmes/education-and-ecumenical-formation/ete/ecumenical-covenant-on-theological-education.

———. *Nairobi to Vancouver, 1975–1983: Report of the Central Committee to the Sixth Assembly of the World Council of Churches*. Geneva: WCC, 1983.

World Missionary Conference, 1910, *Report of Commission V: The Training of Teachers*. Edinbugh: Oliphant, Anderson & Ferrier, 1910.

Young, Curtis J. "Transformational Learning in Ministry." *Christian Education Journal* series 3, vol. 10, no. 2 (2013): 322–38.

Zizioulas, John. "The Theological Problem of 'Reception.'" *Bulletin Centro Pro Unione* 26 (Fall 1984): 3–6.

Index

Alfeyev, Hilarion, 23, 29–30
Anglican Consultative Council, 20
Anglican-Roman Catholic International Commission, 13, 16, 19–20, 62, 97, 112
Association of Theological Schools in the United States and Canada, 39–40, 92, 134–36, 140
Arthur Turner Training School, 91
Atlantic School of Theology, 38, 91, 135
Avis, Paul, 163

baptism, 14, 60, 68, 75, 83, 119, 121, 133, 143–47, 154, 156
Baptism, Eucharist, and Ministry, 19, 96–97, 112, 144
Bossey Ecumenical Institute, 11, 36, 74–82, 84, 86, 89, 98, 104, 114–15, 136–37
Budde, Mitzi J., 98, 104, 107, 126–42, 148, 154, 157

Canadian Centre for Ecumenism, 51
Church of England, 54, 152
Clifford, Catherine, 83, 104
College of Emmanuel and St. Chad, 91
Commission on Faith and Order, 13, 17, 30, 144, 146
Conference of Theological Seminaries, 37, 40
Congar, Yves, 15–17, 22, 29, 132
Council of Florence, 22–24, 27
COVID-19, 134, 164–65

Dowd, Thomas, 90–91, 103, 158

Ecumenical common prayer/worship, 36, 43, 51, 54, 57, 61, 68–69, 75–76, 83–84, 87, 90, 100, 103, 113–14, 119, 130, 132, 139
Ecumenical Directory, 42, 48–49, 52–53, 87
Ecumenical friendships, 51, 69, 84–85, 113–14, 130
Ecumenical Patriarchate of Constantinople, 35
Ecumenical reception, 2–4, 6, 8, 10, 14, 16–31
Ecumenical shared ministries, 54, 120, 143, 149–52, 154, 156, 165
Episcopal Church, 54, 127, 133, 149
Evangelical Lutheran Church in America, 127, 133, 141, 149
Evangelical Lutheran Church in Canada, 6, 21, 98–99, 112, 142–43, 147–48, 150–51, 156
Extracurricular activities, 50–52, 68–69, 80–86, 89, 93–94, 99–101, 108, 113–14, 118, 122, 129, 134, 139, 157, 160

Field education, 99, 103, 130–31, 142
Freire, Paolo, 70–71, 87

General Synod of the Anglican Church of Canada, 5–6, 21, 45, 140, 155–56, 166

Growing Together in Unity and Mission, 55–56, 59–68, 121–22, 143, 152–53

Hayes, Alan, 106–7, 140
Huron College, 91

Indigenous peoples, 160–61
Initiation into Christ, 143–47
Intergroup contact theory, 162
International Anglican-Roman Catholic Commission on Unity and Mission, 55–56, 58, 143, 152
Inter-Anglican Standing Commission on Ecumenical Relations, 19–20, 53

Joint Declaration on the Doctrine of Justification, 23
Joint Working Group between the Roman Catholic Church and the World Council of Churches, 7–8, 42–44, 89, 93, 96–98, 110, 132, 137, 142, 153, 163

Kasper, Walter, 52, 56–58, 121–22, 146
Kinnamon, Michael, 7, 50, 82, 99

Lund Principle, 5–6, 58–59, 68, 121

Mannion, Gerard, 26, 30
MacDonald, Mark, 161
master of divinity, 49, 92, 103, 135, 155
McGill University, 37–38
Mennonites, 5, 39, 101, 150
Mezirow, Jack, 72–76, 79–81, 86–87, 114–15, 118, 122–23, 130, 137
Montreal Diocesan Theological College, 50, 91
Montreal School of Theology, 38
Moravian Church, 5, 133, 141
Murray, Paul D., 58

null curriculum, 131–32

O'Gara, Margaret, 28, 50, 71, 83–88, 132, 136
online learning, 49, 95, 127, 134–40, 154, 160–61, 164–65

Osmer, Richard, 10–11, 126, 139

Queen's College, 91

Raiser, Konrad, 40
Regan, Jane, 128
Rausch, Thomas P., 16
Rusch, William G., 13–15, 17–18, 21–23, 29
Ryan, Thomas, 19, 29, 52–53, 57–59, 68, 83, 85–86, 121–22, 136–37, 146

Saint Paul University, 39, 49, 91, 135
Second Vatican Council, 7, 15, 18, 25–26, 39, 42, 52, 68, 75, 83, 106, 144, 152, 163

Theological Education in the Anglican Communion, 45
Tillard, Jean-Marie, 18, 25–26, 29
Toronto School of Theology, 39, 48–50, 105–7, 140
Trinity College, 91
Tutu, Desmond, 164
Tveit, Olav Fykse, 164

United Church of Canada, 5, 33, 38–39, 96, 116, 119–21, 143, 150–51, 154

Vancouver School of Theology, 38, 92, 135
Vatican II. *See* Second Vatican Council

Week of Prayer for Christian Unity, 51–52, 61, 83, 90, 95, 100, 103, 113, 120–21, 132
Waterloo Declaration, 97, 112, 142–43, 147–49, 151, 153–54, 156
Willebrands, Johannes, 21, 26–27
Windsor Report, 17
World Council of Churches, 19, 32, 35–37, 41–43, 68, 70, 75, 82, 93, 104, 161, 163–64
World Missionary Conference, 34–35, 37, 68
Wycliffe College, 49, 92, 98, 106, 135

Zizoulas, John, 21

www.ingramcontent.com/pod-product-compliance
Lightning Source LLC
Chambersburg PA
CBHW062044220426
43662CB00010B/1646